Calne -

Gateway to Ancient Wiltshire

Walks through history and landscape

Peter Knight and Sue Wallace

Stone Seeker Publishing
Calne, Wiltshire UK
Honouring ancient wisdom and Mother Earth

Published 2014
by Stone Seeker Publishing,
Wiltshire, England, UK
www.stoneseeker.net
email: stoneseeker@waitrose.com

ISBN: 978-0-9560342-3-6

Also by Peter Knight

Ancient Stones of Dorset - 1996
Sacred Dorset: On the Path of the Dragon - 1998
Dorset Pilgrimages: A Millennium Handbook (with Mike Power) - 2000
Earth Mysteries: An Illustrated Encyclopaedia of Britain (CD-ROM) - 2004
Thirteen Moons: Conversations with the Goddess - 2007 (& 2012 ed.)
The Wessex Astrum: Sacred Geometry in a Mystical Landscape (with Toni
    Perrott) – 2008
West Kennet Long Barrow: Landscape, Shamans and the Cosmos – 2011
The Cerne Giant: Landscape, Gods and the Stargate - 2013

Cover images:
Front cover: Cherhill White Horse; blue plaque in New Road; Cycle Network sign at
    Castlefields Park; Peacock butterfly seen in Calne.
Back cover: stones in avenue, Avebury; Silbury Hill in morning mist; Priestley memorial
    in Calne town centre; Maud's Monument, Bremhill; Black Dog Halt sign.

Cover design: Peter Knight.
All images © P Knight and S Wallace (unless otherwise stated).

Printed and bound by CPI Group (UK) Ltd, Croydon, CR0 4YY

Contents

This book is dedicated to Peter Treloar (RIP)

Calne –
Landscape Setting, Prehistory and History

The town and villages that comprise the Calne Community Area, in North Wiltshire, stand partially on a band of Jurassic Corallian limestone that runs from NE-SW, mostly to the west of the chalk downs. This is a fossiliferous and oolitic limestone and has been quarried locally. Lower ground and river valleys lie mainly on Cretaceous Gault and Jurassic Kimmeridge Clay. Chalk escarpments rise at the southern and eastern part of the area, giving birth to numerous springs and wondrous chalk downland and dry valleys. There are four Sites of Special Scientific Interest (SSSI's) in the Calne area, at Cherhill, Calstone Wellington, King's Play Hill and Stanley.

The River Marden runs roughly E-W through the area, and is joined by the Abberd Brook. The name Calne may have derived from the Celtic 'Col-aun', meaning a current of waters or meeting of rivers, but authorities are uncertain as to whether this is an early name for Abberd Brook or the Marden. As the place name Calstone has the same first element, and Calstone is the source of the Marden, it may have been the latter.

Prehistory

The lives of our prehistoric ancestors are woven into the landscape. There is plenty of evidence that early prehistoric hunters were in the area, such as Mesolithic flints found at Calstone Down, Derry Hill, Sandy Lane and elsewhere, and a settlement in Cherhill parish. Numerous Neolithic finds, such as flints and axe heads, have been found locally; a Neolithic long barrow survives on King's Play Hill, Heddington. A large find of Neolithic flints, hammer-stones and flakes was found near the Marden at Calstone Wellington, and field walking has revealed Neolithic worked flint at Bromham. The Neolithic monuments of Avebury (the world's largest stone circle) and Silbury Hill (the tallest prehistoric mound in Europe) both stand just a few miles to the east.

Numerous Bronze Age burials (shown as 'tumuli' on OS maps) litter the hills around Calne, and one such mound was found just NW of the parish church. A fine group of tumuli survive on Morgan's Hill, which has been shown to be aligned with West Kennet Long Barrow (Knight 2011).

Neolithic flint tool found at Calstone.
(Devizes Museum collection.)

Impressive Iron Age enclosures can be seen at Oldbury Camp, on Cherhill Hill, and at Oliver's Castle (Walks 12 & 14). These 'hillforts' were sacred places long before they were later fortified, as prehistoric burial mounds at both places testify.

The famous alignment known as the St Michael Line passes through the southern extremity of the Calne Community Area, crossing through Oliver's Castle and Roundway Hill (walk 14). This alignment crosses England from Cornwall to East Anglia, and includes notable places such as St Michael's Mount, Glastonbury, and Avebury itself. Another alignment, the Wessex Astrum hexagram, is a further notable landscape feature, which also crosses the area through Lacock, Bowood, Blackland and Cherhill, on its way to Avebury (Knight and Perrot 2008).

Romano-British (Iron Age)

In 1932 Maud Cunnington published a summary of known Roman and Romano-British sites in Wiltshire, showing that there were substantial signs of occupation locally during the Roman period. There was a Roman villa at

Nuthills Farm (walk 9), a settlement at Sandy Lane (Verluccio), and more Roman villas at Bowood and Studley. The Roman road from Londinium (London) to Aqua Sulis (Bath) runs E-W through the area (shown on OS maps), passing over Morgan's Hill and onward through Heddington parish, Stockley, Sandy Lane, Spye Park and Bowden Hill. Smaller Romano-British sites are suggested by coins and building material found at Spray's Farm (Calstone), pottery and coins from Calstone Wellington, and pottery at Blackland. According to the Ancient Monuments Record for Wiltshire, a possible Roman temple site may have stood at Redhill, Derry Hill (grid ref 958708), where worked gold and silver was unearthed. Fragments of

Fragment of Roman floor mosaic found in 1913 in the grounds of Cherhill Manor, depicting an animal running in front of tree.
(Devizes Museum Collection.)

floor mosaic were found at Studley and at Cherhill Manor (image above). In 2009, a speaker at the Roman exhibition held at Calne Heritage Centre raised the question as to why no Roman sites had yet been found in the immediate proximity of the Marden; perhaps they await discovery!

Anglo-Saxon to Medieval

Wansdyke (which means *Wodin's Ditch*, after the god Wodin/Odin) is the massive Saxon bank and ditch that runs 12 miles from Morgan's Hill (walk 14), where it was laid on top of the Roman road, to Savernake Forest. In Saxon times, Calne itself belonged to the King and there was a royal house and a church here. The earliest documentary evidence comes from AD955, when King Eadred or Edred bequeathed Calne to the Minster at Winchester.

The estate was soon back in royal hands, however, and remained so throughout the rest of the Saxon period. A settlement of wattle huts grew around the two storey royal building and became the urban part of the estate, which also included scattered farmsteads; Saxon brooches were found at Calne and Oldbury Hillfort.

In AD978, St Dunstan, the high-ranking Benedictine and soon to be Archbishop of Canterbury, attended the 'Witena-Gemot' or Supreme Council in Calne to justify his controversial re-organisation of the national Church, which proposed the celibacy of clerics and the replacement of secular priests by Benedictine

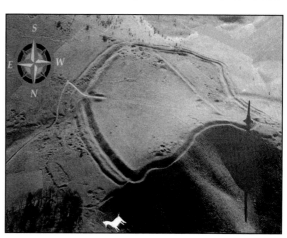

Cherhill Hill, where there is evidence from the Neolithic through to Saxon times.
(Illustration on plaque by A4 at Cherhill).

monks. According to an account written about 1000, during this meeting Dunstan called upon God to support his cause, at which point part of the upper floor collapsed, killing or injuring many of his opponents, whilst Dunstan and his supporters survived the ordeal. This was claimed as 'a miracle' by Dunstan's allies.

There are elevated sites on either bank of the River Marden. The one on the left bank is occupied by the church while it is believed that on the right stood the Saxon King's house, on what is now Castle Hill. Although recent excavations failed to find any emphatic evidence that a medieval fortified site ever stood on Castle Hill, this elevated place does seem a likely site for the royal Saxon house. Both the King's manor and that of the church had the right to hold markets and fairs. That of the church, to the SE, was on the area now known as The Green, whilst that of the King's to the NW is now the area of The Strand, High Street and Market Hill. The church market was held on the Sabbath and there was also a three day fair for the feast of St. Mary Magdalene (July 22). The town fair, granted in 1273, was held on St. Mark's Day, April 25th, although was later changed to May 6th. Both fairs were abolished in 1877. The Domesday Survey of 1086 shows there was a substantial population, possibly around 1,000 on the whole estate, plus seven mills. A hospital was provided on a modest endowment from 1248 until 1546.

Stanley (Stanleigh) Abbey, between Calne and Chippenham, was a Cistercian foundation which grew in size throughout the 12th and 13th centuries, its operations only ceasing with the Dissolution of the Monasteries. It had a fulling mill as early as 1189, making it one of the earliest recorded. No stone now remains in situ, just undulating fields and ditches, all on private property. Access and permission to visit may be obtained from Old Abbey Farm (see Walk 7 for more details and further history). However, the Abbey's original stone gateway now forms the entrance to Spye Park, at Bowden Hill, known locally as Spye Arch (grid ref: 942679 – image right). A medieval hospital associated with Stanley Abbey once stood near Hannah's Wood, west of Derry Hill (grid ref: 942701). Surviving field features of an Augustinian abbey can also be found at Bradenstoke, on the edge of Lyneham, and there is of course Lacock Abbey (walk 9), not far to the west. The importance of Calne

Dragons and a griffin adorn 'Spye Arch' at Spye Park. This was formerly the gateway of Stanley Abbey. (From *The Wessex Astrum*, Knight and Perrott.)

is confirmed by the fact that St Edmund resided here in the 13th century. There were also medieval settlements at Quemerford, and at Beversbrook (north of the Porte Marsh Estate), where features can still be seen in the field, (grid ref c. 004729). The latter was known as Bevresbroc in AD1086, and it had its own chapel, recorded in 1298.

Bowood was a large medieval deer park, and near its southern extremity a 'pillow mound' is shown on OS maps (ref: 981679); these long earthen mounds were built by the Normans as artificial rabbit warrens. Cherhill once had a huge Tithe Barn, 110ft long, of which one timber was dated 1425. The celebrated Maud's Causeway was constructed after her death in 1474.

A ford is mentioned in 1491 and there was probably a bridge here in medieval times, although one is not mentioned until the 16th century. Calne stands on the important London to Bristol coaching road. Two old milestones at Quemerford still inform the traveller it is 87 and 86 miles to London; the one illustrated above is outside no. 123 London Road. Others survive, such as west of the Divine café at Cherhill, at Bowden Hill (image p. 116), and two others at Beckhampton (p. 184). An important turnpike road to Bath ran through Bowood, Sandy Lane and Lacock (Walk 9).

In 1340, a serious fire destroyed many of the earlier timber-framed houses, which were then replaced by dwellings built of local limestone rubble with interior timber walls. The central market place probably remained open until the late 17th century but by 1728 most of it had been built over. Whilst there was minor encroachment upon The Green, this remained a largely open area.

Forward To Modern Times

In 1643, during the English Civil War, the Battle of Roundway took place. The fields of battle were within the southern edge of the Calne area, with further skirmishes occurring in Calne in 1645. The Tounson almshouses in Kingsbury St were built in 1682 for needy widows (walk 5).

By the 14th century Calne was a centre for cloth-making, originally producing undyed cloth. In 1331 Edward III gave permission for Flemish weavers and dyers to come to Calne. St Mary's church was rebuilt by the donations from rich clothiers and wool merchants in the 15th century (and is among a minority of medieval churches that are Grade I listed). Wool was the chief industry in the area during the 17th century, the Chivers family of Quemerford being the most important clothiers – one of whom was knighted by Charles I. Some twenty cloth mills were spread along the Marden, and from the mid-18th century the leading lights in this industry were the Bailey family. At the end of the 18th century there were fourteen clothiers and two woolstaplers in the town, but the industry was to decline with the onset of the 19th century, when some mills turned to grinding corn; from the 1850's to 1870's paper was made at Quemerford Mill.

As well as the many watermills, there were at least two full-scale factory mills, at Horsebrook and Quemerford (walk 6), although only Quemerford Mill seems to have had a steam engine. There were excellent wool workshops on the eastern side of The Green, at 'Weaver's House' and nos. 8 and 9. The industry was declining from the mid 1820s and by 1835 there were only three sites remaining. By 1848 cloth-making in Calne had ceased and the waterwheel of Upper Quemerford Mill was finally removed in 1932.

The surviving chimney and buildings of Lower Quemerford Mill, remnants of the former glory days of Calne's wool trade.

The town expanded in the late 17th and early 18th centuries, with a fair amount of rebuilding, such as the Catherine Wheel Inn and a market house. Later building extended the urban area along roads leading out of the town. There are good examples of 18th century houses in Patford Street, North Street and Castle Street. The town acquired two fire engines in 1748, gifted to the town by its members of Parliament.

The Harris factory, which once dominated the centre of Calne and in it's heyday employed over 2000 workers. (Image on display in Calne Heritage Centre.)

The Wilts and Berks Canal served the town from 1802 to 1901, eventually reaching the Town Mill by canalising the River Marden. A wharf and warehouse was built and New Road was created on the eastern bank, linking London Road to the Port Bridge over the Marden. Canal trade ceased in 1901, following the collapse of the aqueduct at Stanley.

The town flourished in the 19th century, during which nonconformist chapels, a free church and six schools were built. A workhouse was built around 1847, a new Town Hall erected on the site of the Town Mill in 1886, and a new hospital in 1888. Commercial buildings including shops and inns were rebuilt, while a new bank was built in the 1870's.

Harris's factory was the culmination of a local bacon-curing industry that had been the chief source of employment from the latter part of the 19th century. From the second half of the 18th century the Harris brothers, John and Henry, each developed their own businesses, the descendants of whom eventually amalgamated in 1888 as C. & T. Harris & Co. Production included bacon, sausages, lard, pies and tinned meats, and in its heyday Harris's employed over 2,000 people. The factory generated its own electricity and from 1926-1948 the Borough Council used this supply for the town. Queen Mary visited the Harris factory in 1941, to encourage the war effort.

Most other industries were small, but there was a substantial iron foundry and engineering works, Maundrell Ltd, in Horsebrook. From 1888 they manufactured a range of items, including pumps, lorry parts, railings, and equipment for Harris's. The foundry closed in 1957 but engineering continued on the site until the 1990s. Some of Maundrell's drain covers can still be seen around Calne (image p. 83). There was also a gasworks in Horsebrook, providing town lighting from 1838 to 1939.

Successive Marquises of Lansdowne of Bowood have been influential on Calne since the 1760's, although it was not until 1890 that Bowood was included in the parish of Calne Without. The Lansdownes played host to philosophers, writers and scientists. In the 18th century the chemist Joseph Priestley was librarian at Bowood and discovered oxygen there in 1774 (Walk 8); he also lived on The Green in Calne for several years (Walk 5). Other visitors included US President Benjamin Franklin and poet Dr. Samuel Johnson. In the 18th–early 19th century Calne itself provided accom-modation for writer Charles Lamb and poet/philosopher Samuel Taylor Coleridge. King and Queen Alexandra

The once-bustling railway station at Calne.

stayed at Bowood in 1907.

In 1863 a single-track railway line was opened between Chippenham and Calne, with a station on the edge of the town, marked today by Station Road. At one stage there was 41 station staff. In 1873 a private line was built to Bowood House, and there were also stops at Black Dog Halt and Studley Bridge (see Walk 7). The line was closed in 1965 and Calne station was demolished shortly after; the track was taken up in 1967.

There was very little expansion between 1900 and 1920 but over the next 50 years Calne Council built around 1,700 houses. Two industrial estates were created between 1960 and 1980. After the closure of Harris's factory in 1983, a charitable organisation called the Calne Project was set up to regenerate the town. The factory site in the town centre was cleared and new housing built, plus a new shopping development.

Romantic old drawing of a very rural-looking Calne, with cows and sheep, at the time of the canals, with lock in the centre.

Calne is still uncovering its heritage. In 2007, divers found the lost hamlet of Mannings Hill at the bottom of Bowood Lake; Calne Heritage Centre, an excellent hub for local history, has opened in the old library; blue plaques have been hung around Calne; and excavations were recently carried out on Castle Hill.

Whilst embracing its colourful history, Calne is making great strides to 're-invent' itself, striving to ensure that Calne moves with the times, whilst at the same time preserving its cultural heritage and environmental diversity. From the roots of the past grow the branches of the future.

Walking Through History

The Past All Around Us

When we started work on this handbook, we had but an inkling that we would uncover much more than met the eye around Calne and its surrounding landscapes. For many years we have been walking the Wiltshire countryside and visiting ancient sites. One of us had previously published books describing sacred sites and their placement within their extended landscape. And we already knew that Calne had a long industrial heritage, such as the wool trade, Harris's factory, and Calne's former canal and railway links. But we were genuinely surprised at what survives in and around Calne when one walks around with keen eyes. This is complemented by the ancient relics in the area, dating from the Neolithic through to Roman, Saxon and medieval times. History, and indeed prehistory, really is all around us.

Relics of industrial heritage pepper Calne and blue plaques help locate where historical events have happened, or where personalities resided. Locally, an old sundial, a granite fountain, a giant barometer, a waterwheel, coaching arches, listed buildings, stunning churches and ancient sunken tracks all reveal themselves to the enquiring mind. All these and more help us to connect with our cultural heritage. Winston Churchill once said that the more we look back in history, the more able we are to move forward. History helps create community, and a sense of belonging. We would add that relating to one's local *landscape* is equally vital, giving us roots with which to connect with this beautiful area of North Wiltshire.

Calne – Hub for Ancient North Wiltshire

Calne may not be as famous, or as well-frequented by tourists, as some of its neighbouring towns, such as Lacock, Marlborough or Devizes, and yet it is ideally situated from which to visit many places in North Wiltshire and beyond. Calne is perfectly placed as a hub to visit the Roman spa at Bath, the ancient monuments of Stonehenge and Avebury, the abbey at Lacock, and as a starting point to walk and cycle across the magnificent chalk scarps and downland of North Wiltshire. Miles of public footpaths, bridleways and cycle routes pass through the Calne Community Area, linking rambler and cyclist alike to stunning scenery, including SSSI's and World Heritage sites. It is along these quiet tracks that one may experience something that can be rare nowadays — the sound of silence.

Walk On the Wild Side

Walking continues to grow as a recreational activity, as 'rambling' has reached an all time popularity. The benefits of walking for health and well-being are well documented, and the need to herald such benefits is greater than ever as obesity levels in the UK reach record levels. Rambling gets us out into the fresh air, away from TV and PC, and exercises lungs, muscles and heart alike; and, unlike most other pleasures, walking is free!

We may be taken out of our comfort zone, venturing into realms anew, to trek across unfamiliar landscapes. We meet Nature in the raw, encountering quiet streams and dark woods, deer and badgers, red kites and water voles, orchids and butterflies, stone circles and long barrows, in varying weather conditions. We may push ourselves harder physically and mentally than is required during a visit to the local shops. Although walking with others is satisfying, as one interacts with like minds, solitary walking is also to be recommended; here one is free from chit-chat and distractions, free to follow one's own way and act on one's own intuition. This process could readily be described as 'sauntering for the Soul' (Knight and Power, 2000), as one's mind is freed to expand beyond the confines of everyday life. And it is not just the body that is liberated during a long walk, but the spirit also. The concept of pilgrimage is very ancient; this is an act of consciously journeying to a sacred place, for the betterment of one's faith and spirituality. It is often quoted that the journey is as important as the destination; this is so true. What one encounters en route may result in the most meaningful experience of a pilgrimage, as one is invited to look not only upon unknown landscapes, but also within our heart and soul.

The rhythmic action of walking is very meditative, and one may come to realise that life's journeys are really interior. The Aborigines of Australia famously go 'walkabout' as part of their initiations, as they purposefully separate themselves from their peers, seeking solitude to connect with the

land, the ancestors – and themselves. Any landscape is never merely a region to be crossed, but rather a place that can be experienced. Whether we follow Neolithic pilgrims to Avebury, walk in the footsteps of rural folk along Maud's Causeway, or simply wish to gander flank, every byway has the potential to be a Yellow Brick Road, full of latent potential, surprise – and magic.

The Country Code: Please ensure you respect the countryside; close gates after yourself; keep dogs on lead near livestock; do not walk across crops; take nothing but photos; leave nothing behind except footprints.

17

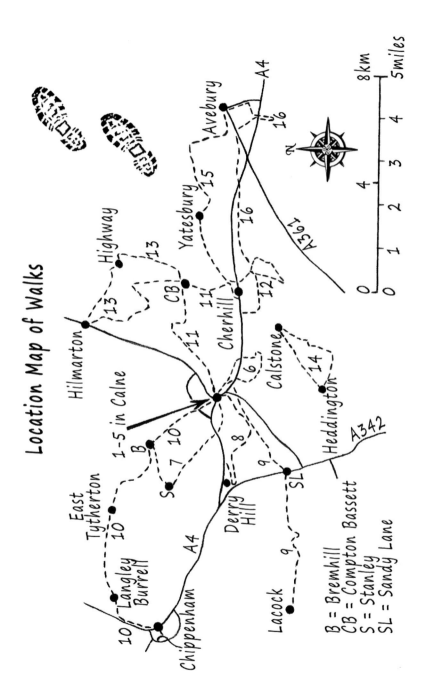

Location Map of Walks

Highway
13
Yatesbury
15
Avebury
A4
16
16
CB
11
Cherhill
12
11
13
Hilmarton
6
Calstone
14
1-5 in Calne
B
7 10
Heddington
S
8
A342
East Tytherton
10
9
Derry Hill
SL
Langley Burrell
10
A4
9
10
Chippenham
Lacock
A361
N
0 1 2 3 4 5miles
0 4 8km

B = Bremhill
CB = Compton Bassett
S = Stanley
SL = Sandy Lane

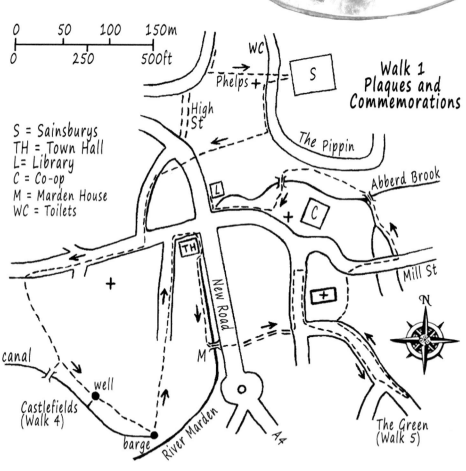

**Walk 1
Plaques and
Commemorations**

S = Sainsburys
TH = Town Hall
L = Library
C = Co-op
M = Marden House
WC = Toilets

0   50   100   150m
0   250   500ft

WC
Phelps
S
High St
The Pippin
Abberd Brook
L
C
Mill St
TH
New Road
M
canal
well
Castlefields
(Walk 4)
barge
River Marden
A4
N
The Green
(Walk 5)

Walk 1.

Plaques and Commemorations

Summary of Walk 1

Distance: 2km (1.25 miles).
Circular or linear: linear, but end is close to start point.
Start point: Curzon St, Calne (grid ref: 997712).
End point: Library, Calne.
Degree of difficulty: very easy walking, all on tarmac/pavements.
Seasonal/weather restrictions: none.
Boots/wellies required: no.
Public transport back to start point: not applicable.
Wheelchair accessible: yes, except Proclamation Steps (short detour).
Refreshments and toilets: several cafes and pubs locally, plus WC.
OS Explorer Map: 156.

This walk includes most of the blue plaques and other commemorations to be seen around Calne town centre, and demonstrates a little of the area's rich heritage. The round blue plaques were installed in 2000 by the Calne Civic Society and bear the Calne coat of arms.

The start point is in Wood St, where a blue plaque over shop no. 9 tells us that the building was a Quaker Meeting House from 1829-1874. It was built by the Fry family from Bristol, at the cost of £491, and seated up to 150 people. Quaker meetings are recorded in Calne in 1660.

From here walk the short distance south to the entrance of Phelps Parade. Two bronze pigs, made by local sculptor Richard Cowdy, are a 1979 commemoration of Calne's long-standing association with the Harris family, whose pork factory dominated the town until its demolition in 1984-5.

(This bronze is part of Calne's Art Trail, a leaflet of which can be found at the Visitor Information Centre at Bank House). From here, walk through Phelps Parade to the Zion Chapel, which bears the date of 1836. Set into the ground in front of the door is a plaque informing us that 64 'departed souls' were buried here from 1836-78. Now cross to the entrance of Sainsbury's. On the forecourt is another bronze work, also by Richard Cowdy, depicting two sheep, celebrating Calne's heritage as a hub for the

Outside Sainsbury's, artwork celebrates crop circles and Calne's wool industry.

wool industry. Around the forecourt are circular, cobbled features by David Reeves, which represent the mysterious crop circles, of which Wiltshire is the acknowledged international centre.

From here walk south down The Pippin, turn right across the car park and exit at the far end through Harris Court, named after the pig factory family. Cross the main road to the off licence and the steps of Market Hill. This is the site of the old Town Hall, prior to its demolition in 1883. The steps are known as Buckeridge Steps, after a long-standing local family business; here a blue plaque proclaims, 'Opposite stood the stocks and the 17th century Town Hall'. Nearby is an unusual Indian Bean tree, one of three in the town centre commemorating Calne's twinning associations.

At the top of the steps turn left along Castle Street and proceed to the next junction, where you will see a blue plaque headed 'Castle House' directly opposite. The text begins with, 'Here Was Anciently A Castle...', a 1670 quote from antiquarian John Aubrey, who reasoned that a castle once stood on the site of the present building. Castle Hill may indeed have been the site of a Saxon King's house, and also possibly of a later tower. Castle House dates from 1770, built by Robert Adams in the Neo Classical Style, but was recently rebuilt following a fire. The entrance pillars are late 18th century and are in fact listed.

Continue west along Castle Street and, not far beyond Chaveywell Court, take the track on the left. This descends to Castlefields Park and at the bottom is a small jetty from which to view the bridge that spans the former Wilts and Berks Canal (image p. 60). On the east side of the bridge can be seen a plaque celebrating the re-opening of Chavey Well Wharf by the Earl of Shelburne on June 11th 1989.

Walk east alongside the canal, and Chavey Well (or Chaveywell) is soon encountered. This natural spring issues pure, refreshing water to this day. The plaque here tells how the waters remained pure during typhoid epidemics in 1880 and 1890.

The plaque telling of the pure waters of Chavey Well (also see image p. 58).

From here continue along path that follows the canal until the new narrow boat installation is reached. This is dealt with in more detail on the Castlefields walk (Walk 4, and Colour Plate 5). For now we can examine the

Plaque to Walter Goodall George on the north side of the Town Hall.

excellent information boards which tell of the canal's history. The canal was built between 1795 and 1810, but traffic ceased in 1901 following the collapse of the aqueduct at Stanley. It is now the longest stretch of derelict canal in the country. The Wilts and Berks Canal Partnership is now actively restoring the canal.

From the narrow boat go through the black gates, straight ahead under the arch, and down to end of Patford Street. Turn right to the Town Hall. On the north side can be seen a plaque celebrating the sporting efforts of Calne athlete Walter Goodall George (1858–1943), who was born nearby. He incredibly held the record for the mile from 1886 to 1915. The plaque was unveiled in 1986 to commemorate the centenary of his record.

Blue plaque next to Marden House.

From here one can see two more of the Indian Bean trees celebrating Calne's twinning associations (one outside Bank House, the other on the corner by the Lansdowne Strand Hotel). Next, go around the front of Town Hall to the bridge, from under which issues the River Marden. On the south side is a blue plaque telling of the Wharf, which opened in 1802 as the terminus of the Calne section of the Wilts and Berks canal. If you continue along the footpath between the river and the gardens you will soon see a large stone on the grass on the right. Although difficult to make out now, this is an earlier commemoration of the Wharf.

Continue along this path, turning left toward the main road over the next bridge. Next to an old water pump, is the next blue plaque (images above and below), celebrating the London to Bath coach road. There were

turnpike gates at either end of the town, both marked on a 1773 map. In its heyday, this main highway was used by up to 400 horse-driven coaches a day. New Road was built in 1801 by Calne Turnpike Trust. The plaque adds that, 'The pump was used to lay the dust'.

This plaque is also a good opportunity to examine at eye-level Calne's coat of arms, which was granted in 1950: The feathers refer to the fact that Calne was formerly part of the Duchy of Cornwall. The ecclesiastical emblems in the

Plaque and pump celebrating Calne's importance as a coaching stop.

crest recall the disastrous events of AD 978, the so-called 'Miracle of St Dunstan', recorded in the Anglo-Saxon Chronicle. The boars represent the pork industry that once dominated the town. It is said that the industry developed here because pigs reared in Ireland were landed at Bristol and then herded across England on drovers' roads to Smithfield in London,

Blue plaque dedicated to Samuel Taylor Coleridge on Bentley House, Church St.

The plaque to Jan Ingen Housz above the post box at Church House, Church St.

passing through Calne. The words at the foot of the coat of the arms are 'Faith, Work, Service'. Now cross the main road, bear right and then left down Ivy Walk, under the 'Kerry Crescent' arch with its ornate decoration. At Church Street turn left. House no. 19 bears the following inscription over the door: *The Old Butchers Arms c.1865-1985.* The wrought iron support for the former pub sign survives. Continue along to Bentley House. The blue plaque is in honour of Samuel Taylor Coleridge. He was a leading romantic poet, who stayed here from 1814 to 1816 whilst writing his *Biographia Literaria,* as a guest of Dr Page, then Mayor of Calne.

Cross over the road to the post box, which stands outside Church House, a building shown on a 1728 map. On its wall you will see a blue plaque commemorating the Dutch scientist Dr Jan Ingen Housz (1730-1799). He pioneered

Original plaque telling how Dr Tounson built the almshouses in Kingsbury St.

studies into the inoculation against smallpox; he also repeated Dr Joseph Priestley's experiments, finding that it was sunlight acting upon the plants that produced oxygen - the process now known as photosynthesis. He was invited to Bowood in 1779, where he lived until his death. He is buried in the Lansdowne vault in St Mary's.

From here, walk back along Church St, skirting the churchyard until you reach the War Memorial. This is unusual in that the shaft is graced with an elegant sword.

From here turn left into Kingsbury Street and on the bend will be found Dr Tounson's Almshouses, one of the oldest buildings in Calne. An old plaque

Proclamation Steps in Mill Street, the scene of announcements in times gone by.

tells how the almshouses were built by Dr Tounson, vicar of Bremhill, after the Civil War for the housing of elderly widows of the parish. He had lost his living during the war but was later reinstated by Charles II, and donated the almshouses in gratitude.

Continue into The Green, crossing over the road until you reach the blue plaque at Weaver's House (image p. 74). The plaque tells us that the building was once a 'wool trade workshop'. We shall return to this building as well as look at others on The Green on Walk 5. Retrace your steps to the churchyard wall and take the narrow passage on your right, which skirts around the east side of the church to reach Mill Street. Descend

The plaque celebrating Joseph Priestley at Doctor's Pond.

Proclamation Steps, to find an attendant rectangular blue plaque on the wall of Proclamation House. This plaque was installed in 1977 in honour of the Queen's Silver Jubilee (see image p.80 and Colour Plate 2). The inscription tells us that 'from time immemorial' Royal Proclamations and other important announcements were made here. It was also along Mill Street that 17th century plague victims were carried, to be buried on the other side of the Marden behind what is now Anchor Road.

This plaque on the bridge over the River Marden commemorates Harris's.

From here walk east along Mill Street, where two bridges take you over the mill run and the Marden proper. In the doorway of the old mill, formerly known as Low's Mill, are mounted two, old granite mill stones (image p. 39). Turn left down the path that follows the Marden and just before the footbridge note the small rectangular plaque low down to the left (image above). This proclaims that this part of the river, where the Marden is joined by the waters of Abberd Brook, is known as Doctor's Pond, another epitaph to Dr Joseph Priestley, who discovered oxygen whilst working at Bowood House.

Local folklore says that he carried out some of his experiments near this spot. From here go over the footbridge and cross the car park diagonally, in the direction of the recycling bins. Turn left when you get into the neighbouring car park, heading diagonally down to the footbridge. On the west side of the bridge is fixed another blue plaque, celebrating Harris's bacon factories (image previous page). The inscription says that the factories were, 'hemming in both sides of the River Marden', and were, '... the prime industry in Calne'.

The modern wall mural depicting some of Calne's traditions, buildings and monuments.

Cross over the bridge, which spans fast flowing waters during wet weather, and in front of you is a large modern mural, filling most of the back of a building. This colourful work of art shows scenes of local relevance, such as the Cherhill White Horse, the Lansdowne Monument, The Head, Harris's, sheep, pigs, the Lansdowne Arms, and St. Mary's. It was created by pupils of John Bentley School and is one of several modern art initiatives around Calne, some more of which we will soon see.

Priestley art installation next to the river in Church St.

Continue around the path until a seating area is reached on your left. This is another of Calne's public art installations, designed by David Reeves and the Calne Artists' Group. The seating encircles a floor mosaic in honour of Dr Priestley (image left). Various brass images (sadly now tarnished) depict how oxygen is essential to all living things, and an image of the good doctor is at the centre (see image next page, and on the back cover). Patterns of petals are set into the ground, and letters represent the

Inset carvings in the river wall near the Library.

elements, the names of which are inscribed around the perimeter. In between the seating are smaller mosaics depicting animals, with some appropriately profound verses beneath. The floor plaque tells of Priestley's achievements in the latter half of the 18th century whilst he was resident in Calne.

Follow the pavement

towards the Library and the traffic lights, with the Marden on your right. Go through the flood gate and stand by the river bank. On the opposite side of the waters you will see various images set into the riverside wall. These reliefs were created by Richard Cowdy and Vivien ap Rhys Price of the Calne Artists' Group, and reflect the 'Breath of Life' theme, reinforcing the life-bestowing qualities of oxygen, the discovery of which is so closely associated with Calne through Dr Priestley. A rabbit, a person blowing a feather, birds, a beetle and a mouse are amongst the images to be seen. Other ceramic glazed tiles nearby similarly reflect the essential nature of oxygen, designed by pupils from St. Edmund's School, under the direction of David Reeves.

Joseph Priestley bronze relief near the river, the hub of an impressive art installation. (See also back cover).

The flood gates here give us a reminder of past flooding in Calne. Big floods swept through the town in the 1870s, and in 1920, 1932 and 1934. From here continue towards the Library. One soon encounters The Head, perhaps Calne's most striking and thought-provoking modern art work. This was born out of a competition initiated by the Town Mayor in 2000, who called for a sculpture to celebrate the new millennium. The winner was sculptor Rick Kirby and his theme reflects both the past and future of

Calne; the front of the head is complete and symbolises the past, whereas the back is incomplete, its lattice representing the future and the 'challenges of the technological age ahead'. The sculpture was unveiled in December 2001 by HM The Queen, who described it as 'interesting'.

On the corner of the pavement, just beyond the benches, one will see patterns of leaves on the ground, designed by David Reeves, which snake up towards the library entrance. They end at a bronze relief, made by Vivien ap Rhys Pryce, of the head of Jan Ingen Housz, who you may recall was the

The Head, Calne's controversial sculpture, a millennium work by Rick Kirby.

discoverer of photosynthesis. His plaque is on Church House and he was buried within St. Mary's Church. The star shape around the head represents the sun and various granite and ceramic inserts further enforce the story of the photosynthesis process of plants. The leaves also link to the leaves of the pages of books within the adjacent library. A plaque nearby tells of Housz's achievements.

This walk concludes at Calne Library, which houses a fine selection of books relating to Calne's history, as well as older large-scale maps of the area, which proved a very useful resource to us. Underfoot as one enters the building is a quote from Tennyson: 'KNOWLEDGE COMES, BUT WISDOM LINGERS'.

The bronze head of scientist Jan Ingen Housz, the discoverer of photosynthesis.

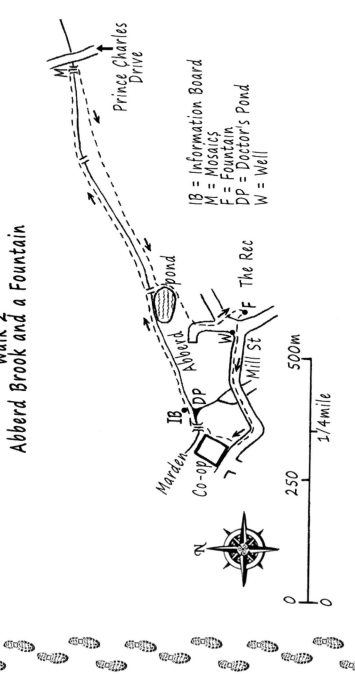

Walk 2
Abberd Brook and a Fountain

IB = Information Board
M = Mosaics
F = Fountain
DP = Doctor's Pond
W = Well

Walk 2.
Abberd Brook and a Fountain

```
Summary of Walk 2

Distance: 2 km (1.25 miles).
Circular or linear: circular.
Start and end point: the Co-op supermarket, Mill St.
Degree of difficulty: very easy walking, mostly on pavements.
Seasonal/weather restrictions: none.
Boots/wellies required: no.
Public transport back to start point: not applicable.
Wheelchair accessible: mostly, except around the pond (steps).
Refreshments and toilets: several cafés and pubs locally, and WC.
OS Explorer Map: 157.
```

This walk is a gentle one that takes in the lower parts of the Abberd Brook and returns via Calne's old fountain and Mill Street.

From the Co-op entrance, cross the footbridge over the Marden and turn right. Doctor's Pond is on the right (see p. 26-27), and ahead you will soon come to a new information board, which was instigated by Friends of Abberd Brook, a collection of enthusiastic volunteers who in recent years have actively worked with the local community on conservation projects along the stream (www.fabrook.org.uk). It states that their aim is to, 'increase the biodiversity of the area, and to create a pleasant green corridor for the residents of Calne'. This informative, well-illustrated board documents the diverse wildlife and flora, which includes water voles, herons, toads, kingfishers, and many species of wildflowers. Abberd Brook is one of the tributaries of the River Marden and has its source about three miles

The information board describing the wildlife of Abberd Brook, and conservation work being carried out along its course.

away at Compton Bassett, which we will see in walk 13, as we will pass over it. We also cross the upper reaches of the brook in Walk 11.

Follow the path that runs alongside the brook, immediately noting the old orchard in the garden to your left, and continue through wildlife-friendly areas, passing mainly under willows. We saw a kingfisher here on one of our walks. Keep your eyes open for water voles, as well as their holes in the banks which can be seen where undergrowth is sparse. You will see a pond across stream, but ignore this for now, continuing along the path, and ignoring any bridges and stepping stones further on. Follow the path as it skirts behind houses, until you come to an underpass which goes under Prince Charles Drive.

The blue plaque marking the unveiling of the mosaics on 1st October 2011.

The mosaics in the underpass by Abberd Brook - an inspiring local community project.

The underpass is wonderfully adorned with ceramic mosaics commissioned by Friends of Abberd Brook and designed by artists Gill and David Reeves and eight pupils from Priestley School. The accompanying plaque was unveiled 1st October 2011, and the project is an inspiring example of what local communities can achieve. The colourful and intricate ceramics depict local wildlife, such as birds, fish, insects and butterflies.

Now cross the footbridge next to underpass, turn right and walk down-stream following the brook. Where the path veers left away from the stream, carry straight ahead across the grass, passing near to two oaks. More oaks will soon be encountered, and you should continue on by these, and over the pipe that channels water of a tributary of the brook. Continue to follow the

The pond next to Abberd Brook is a tranquil place.

brook until the large pond is visible in front of you, and go down the small flight of steps to this tranquil spot. Walk along the boardwalk, passing over a damp area where a spring feeds the pond, and ascend the steps on the other side. At the top turn right, where you have a nice view of the church tower, and walk across the grassy area in the direction of the church. Turn left when you get to the road and head towards the iron gates of the Recreation Ground, our next destination. The Rec, as it is known locally, was opened in 1891 and paid for by Thomas Harris, who also provided the caretakers house next to the gates. Note the six fine copper beeches in the distance across the grounds. This great local amenity annually plays host to CalneFest, which continues a long tradition of local events held here, such as maypole dancing in the 1920's.

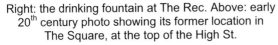

Right: the drinking fountain at The Rec. Above: early 20th century photo showing its former location in The Square, at the top of the High St.

Just this side of the pavilion you will see a drinking fountain, which once stood at the top of the High Street (image above and Colour Plate 3). This used to be called The Square and old photos from the early 1900's show the fountain in situ there. The fountain has a grey stone base, basins of pink Shap granite (from Cumbria) and a cast iron top, which once supported a gas lamp and a road sign directing travellers to both Bath and London.

Another fountain at The Rec, now lost, is shown in a photo from WW1, which shows a structure with four elaborate pillars supporting an arched roof, bearing an inscription: 'The Fear of the Lord is A Fountain of Life'.

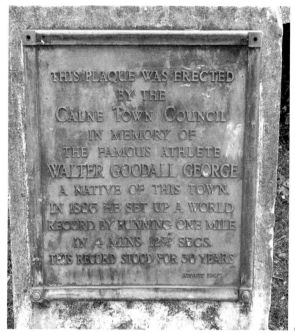

Walking back towards the iron gates note the plaque set on a stone, which is mounted on the ground to your left. This is dated 1948 and commemorates the achievements of Calne athlete Walter Goodall George, who held the world record for the mile from 1886 to 1915. George also held more than thirteen world records for running at the time; he still holds the distinction of having held the mile record longer than anyone else. His 1886

Plaque to Calne athlete Walter Goodall George, near the entrance to The Rec.

record of 4 minutes and 12¾ seconds is recorded on the plaque. You may recall that another plaque honouring him is mounted on the Town hall (see image p. 22), where a picture of the athlete hangs in the foyer.

Now cross over the road to the old well you can see set into the wall of the Old Coaching House. Note also the stone horse's heads either side of the gate. Pass the entrance and go down the hill (Mill Street), following the old wall, and noting the pillared entrance to the Old Vicarage (formerly Parsonage House). Due to a lack of room for his family at premises on The Green, later known as Priestley House, Dr Priestley stayed at Parsonage House between 1775-1780, whilst in the employment of Lord Shelburne, and a

The Old Coaching House with horses on the gate and a
well inset into the old wall.

fish pond either in the grounds or close by may have been the actual 'Doctor's Pond', where the good doctor reputedly saw bubbles of air rising up through the water. Continue down Mill Street to Calne Mill by the bridge (now a private residence), where two old millstones can be viewed in the doorway. One still has metal inserts in the middle, where it was attached to turning machinery. This was known as Lows Mill, and is sandwiched between two flows of the waters. There was a mill standing here in 1341, and is named as Lows Mill in 1723 and was part of Eastman Street Manor in the 18th and 19th centuries. The mill house, on the west side of the mill, was rebuilt in the earlier 19th century. The mill itself was rebuilt in 1857-8, and was used to grind corn until 1866, until later converted for residence. The actor David Hemmings lived here for many years up until his death in December 2003, and his funeral was held at St. Mary's Church. House no. 8 (Pond Cottage) was formerly the miller's house. Candles may have been made in Calne as early as 1669, and a candle factory stood here in Mill Street, recorded in 1828.

Continue down Mill Street, passing Proclamation Steps and its blue plaque on the left (see walk 1 and Colour Plate 2). Further along on the left note the two stone corner protectors, at the two edges of what is a very old shop. Turn right, back to our start point at the Co-op.

One of the millstones in the doorway
of Calne Mill.

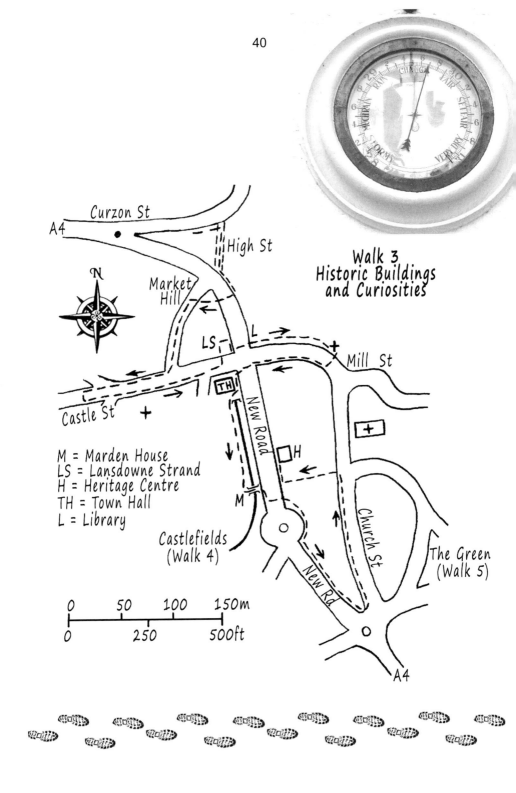

Walk 3
Historic Buildings
and Curiosities

M = Marden House
LS = Lansdowne Strand
H = Heritage Centre
TH = Town Hall
L = Library

Walk 3.
Calne's Historic Buildings and Curiosities

Summary of Walk 3

Distance: 800m (¾ mile).
Circular or linear: linear.
Start point: outside Community Hub, at the top of High St.
End point: Calne Heritage Centre, New Road.
Degree of difficulty: easy walking, mostly on pavements.
Seasonal/weather restrictions: none.
Boots/wellies required: no.
Public transport back to start point: not applicable.
Wheelchair accessible: mostly; ask for access into Heritage Centre.
Refreshments and toilets: several cafés and pubs locally, and WC.
OS Explorer Map: 156.

This walk highlights some of the historic buildings around Calne, as well as unusual or older objects and fittings we discovered. For now, we have excluded St Mary's and The Green, which are dealt with on Walk 5.

We start at the Community Hub, at the top of the High St, a great venue, meeting place and an excellent information centre for local contacts and events.

From the front door of the Hub walk straight ahead (west) along Curzon Street, where you will soon see the date of 1617 on the side of one of the buildings, making it one of the oldest in Calne.

From here, retrace your steps. Adjacent to the parking area at the top of the High Street, a drinking fountain used to stand the middle of the road. You can see it in situ in an old photograph (see p. 36); it has since been relocated to The Rec. Turning into the High Street, the building on the corner used to be the post office, and above its solid wooden doors are the Queen's crown and the characters ERII 1953.

Moving down to the King's Arms, we encounter gates formerly used for horses and carriages during Calne's heyday as a stop on the London to Bath road. Either side of the arch, two fascinating advertising boards inform us that *The Eclipse Coach* could be caught here, taking us to such far flung destinations as London, Bath, Bristol, Exeter, Hereford,

One of two old coach service signs outside the King's Arms.

Birmingham, Manchester, and elsewhere, '... except Sundays'. From here continue down the pedestrian area to the shop on the opposite side, which has an arched entrance at the side, leading to an old lane. The shop was Hawkins the butchers and the name can still be made out under the window. Beneath the arch, and under the overhang of the shop, rails and hooks for hanging meat still survive, and the stone corner protectors on the ground testify to horse-drawn deliveries in the past. Above the shop is a

The old arch and hanging meat hooks at the former butchers on the High Street.

very old drain pipe which bears the faint initials DSM, accompanied by two figures wearing fig leaves. Under the arch and down the alley are old outbuildings, which may have been stables or workshops.

Next to the shop is Harris Court, in remembrance of the family that founded the huge pig factory that once stood at the heart of Calne. Cross the road here using the crossing, to the former bank which bears the date of 1836. The building that houses the off licence on the corner is over 300 years old, and was once Buckeridge the grocers and wine merchants, an old, long-running Calne business. The steps running up alongside it are known as Buckeridge Steps and there is a blue plaque on the wall here (see p. 20).

The iron hatch dated 1941 on a building in Market Hill.

At the top of the steps look next to the black door of the unit that is set back. A peculiar black iron hatch is present. It looks like a heavy-duty night deposit access, but we have not been able to ascertain if the building ever was a bank. The ironwork bears the caption 'Maundrell Calne 1941', a

Above: drainpipe dated 1705 on a building in Market Hill. Below: sundial dated 1683 on the rear wall of Dominion House.

product of the old iron foundry in Horsebrook (see Walk 5).

Now cross over to the other side of Market Hill, to West Hill House. It is painted pale red and is currently the office of a solicitor. This building is one of the oldest in Calne and was once a public house, the Bell Inn. Incredibly, a surviving lead drainpipe bracket is dated 1705. Market Hill was recorded in the 13th century, known then as Byestewel.

Walk along Castle Street and look behind the rear of the first building on the left (now Bevirs). Here, on the back wall above the car park, was one of the most surprising finds of our walks around Calne. A slate sundial dated 1683 is mounted on the wall, and although it is somewhat worse for wear, it is an amazing curiosity to find in a Calne side street. The building was once a school, and inside now houses the original 17th century stone fire surround from Castle House.

Nearby is a side street called Quarr Barton, which has a dwelling called the Old Dairy, plus you can see some old buildings belonging to the Order of the Knights of St. John, an organisation founded by monks as the Knights Hospitallers during the Crusades; they were the medical arm of the Knights

Templar, who had a preceptory near Avebury. Their successors are the St. John's Ambulance and St John Trust, the latter of which runs Marden Court nearby. Further along the street note the old gates at the rear of the Lansdowne Hotel. These were storage units and stables of the brewery that once flourished here, which we shall look at soon. For now continue to the end of the street and turn right, passing Castle House (with its blue plaque – see p. 20-21); the original residence was built c.16-17th century, on the site of a much older, possibly fortified, structure.

The rear yard of the Lansdowne Hotel in Victorian times, when the establishment had its own brewery.

As you progress along the lane you will see house names indicating former establishments, such as the Old Dairy, the Old Surgery, and the Coach House. Note the peculiar stone structure on the verge just before Castlefields House. We have been informed that it is an old water trough (see image p. 64). The Baptist Church will soon be reached. The original church was built soon after the Civil War, but was damaged in a violent storm in November 1703. It was repaired, but subsequently the whole building was rebuilt in 1817, and later enlarged. Pre-war photos show that, next to the lane, there was formerly a grand gate, supported by large pillars on both sides,

The barometer on the outside of the Lansdowne Strand Hotel is said to be the largest wheel barometer in the UK.
(Image: Brian R Marshall, Wiki Commons Licence)

and an arch capped with metalwork. This was probably lost during WW2 as part of the war effort. Note the old walls separating the church from Castle House, which reveal several ages of construction and repair, when viewed from Castle House.

We shall return this way again in Walk 4, but for now retrace your steps, head down the steep lane that is Cox's Hill, and go under the arch that leads to the rear yard of the Lansdowne Strand Hotel. The arch and courtyard beyond once served horse drawn coaches in Calne's coaching heyday, and later as an entrance to the brewery. In 1582 the inn was known as The Catherine Wheel, and later, the Lansdowne Arms, and became Calne's principle coaching inn; as many as twenty coaches a day were stopping at the establishment. Compare the view you have to that in the old photo on the previous page. The ramp in the photo survives, and the brewery buildings now serve as hotel

Insurance seal dated 1695 on the outside of the Lansdowne Strand Hotel.

accommodation. A spring used to supply the brewery with water, and still flows into an outhouse at the rear of the property. The Lansdowne Brewery, as it was known, was acquired by C E Fox & Co. in the early 1890s, and supplied not just the inn itself, but was also a wholesaler to other businesses, and even distributed wines and spirits.

Take a wander through the Hotel, where there are many old photos of the premises and Calne on display. In one image a sign shows that the pub once was the headquarters of the Cycle Touring Club. What is now the front entrance and reception used to be an archway and alley where horse drawn coaches would enter and offload their passengers; in the lobby, look for the old barometer dated 1926 and the 'International Timekeeping Device' from the USA. Leaving by the front door turn right, where you will see another of the Indian Bean trees, planted to celebrate Calne's three twinning links. Behind the tree there is a huge barometer on the wall. It is said to be the largest wheel barometer in England and appears on several Victorian photos of the Hotel. A little further along the wall, next to one of the hanging baskets, is a black insurance seal adorned with a lion, dated 1695 (image previous page). After the Great Fire of London in 1666, Nicholas Barbon, a Puritan businessman, pioneered the concept of fire insurance, and this example in Calne shows that cover was by the Lion Fire Insurance Co.

Now cross the traffic lights in the direction of The Head (p. 30) and walk down the Strand into Church Street, passing the River Marden to

Calne Free Church, opened in 1868.

your left. You will soon come to Calne Free Church. It was built by some of Calne's parishioners, who were aggrieved by the new vicar of the parish church. These included members of the Harris family, who had previously worshipped at St. Mary's. Services were held in the Town Hall until the church opened in July 1868. The church is built in the geometrical style, and the tower is adorned with finely carved dragon gargoyles.

Next to Calne Free Church an overhead footbridge used to span the road, connecting the two parts of the Harris pig factory. The Palace/Regent Cinema also stood here until it was demolished in 1970's, to make way for the supermarket and offices. The street hereabouts was once called Butcher's Row, because of the number of butcher's shops; the pork, at least, certainly did not have to come far!

Retrace your steps towards the traffic lights and cross over to Bank House (dated 1901) on the corner. These are the offices of Calne Town Council, and the Visitor and Community Information Centre in reception is well worth a visit. Then cross over to the Town Hall. The previous 'Market Hall' was demolished in 1883 (read details of a plaque on p. 20), and the

present building opened on 27th July 1886. It was built on the site of old Town Mill, or Port Mill, which was demolished in 1884 after being purchased from Lord Lansdowne. A mill is recorded on the site as far back as 1199. The grand tower of the Town Hall was only decided upon after building had commenced,

Calne Town Hall, built on the site of Town Mill, also once housed a police and fire station.

and the whole building cost £9,375. Going around the right side of the Town Hall, you will see the plaque to Walter Goodall George (see image p. 22). The far corner used to be the town's police station. Go through the arch to view double wooden gates on your right, which are those of the Victorian fire house, moved here from new Road in 1888 (see image p. 50). Turn around, and above the arch you will see a coat of arms that once adorned the old Market Hall and was preserved when it was demolished. It belonged to the locally prominent Duckett family, who were, 'Lords of the Hundred of Calne' from 1579-1776.

The coat of arms above the archway at the Town Hall.

King Edward VII and Queen Alexandra visited Calne in 1907 and stayed at Bowood. They delivered an address at the Town Hall on 22nd July, and bunting was hung all around the town in their honour. In 1935, the Town Hall was floodlit and adorned with lights for King George V's Silver Jubilee.

From the front door of the Town Hall, walk along the pavement that follows the west side of the River Marden, until one reaches Marden House directly ahead. This Grade II listed, 18th century building was once the offices of the Wharfinger, the person responsible for the day to day running of The Wharf, the busy loading and unloading terminus of the canal. The first floor was later removed to create a scout hall, and the building was also owned by Harris's, who used it as an archive store. Where the pavement now runs alongside the entrance once stood bicycle racks for workers of the factory. Marden House later fell into a poor state of repair, before being purchased by Wiltshire Council. It is now in the keep of a

Image of the Calne fire pump from around the mid-late 19th century.
This walk visits two of the town's former fire houses.

charitable trust, and offers a great venue for art shows, meetings and music recitals. The gardens at the rear are enclosed and pretty. On the front of the building is a plaque, unveiled by Charles Prince of Wales in 1988, commemorating his visit to the Calne Project and the Marden House Centre. Walk to the main road close by, where there is a blue plaque and an old pump (image p. 23).

From here turn right and walk towards the roundabout, crossing the road using the small crossing island. Continue up New Road until, just before the road junction, you will see an old disused door on the other side (image right). This was the entrance to the old fire engine house, the name of which is still

The door of the old fire engine house on New Road.

The drinking fountain at the corner of The Green and Church Street.

vaguely visible above the door. This housed one pump engine, in one corner of what was then the Poorhouse, until it was re-housed at the Town Hall in 1888. Behind here once stood Woodlands House, a large 19th century Italian-style residence and welfare club, built and owned by the Harris family. It was demolished in 1983, and the present Woodlands Club was built on the site.

Now turn left around the corner at what was, until recently, the King George pub; you can see a delivery hatch, and an archway around the side for receiving clients and deliveries. Note the old drinking fountain on the opposite side, which would have served many a weary traveller and local alike (image above). Unfortunately, the fountain was damaged in recent years. The red telephone kiosk opposite was designed in 1935 and is in fact a Grade II listed monument!

Now walk down Church St, which was once the main route into Calne prior to the building of New Road. This quiet street was once bustling with shops and many of the buildings still display old architecture. If you look at the 1900s view, below, you will see that this street has changed less than most around Calne. No. 41 has a fine old bay window and a blocked coal chute. No. 32 has a grand entrance, with an 18th century pillared portico, which adorns an extension to the original 16th century building. The owner told us that a Victorian extension was then added to the rear. Old shop fronts can

Compare the modern view of Church Street to this photo from the early 1900s. The back of the old school is on the right, with its gate (now blocked off). Several shops and a pub line the left side of the street, and one of the chimneys from the Harris factory belches smoke in the background.

be perceived at nos. 31-37, which are all listed buildings; over two entrances here are large shell-like decorations, finely made from single blocks of local stone, which are in fact faithful copies of earlier versions; these were entrances to the former Constitution Club, the sign of which still adorns the building. The dwelling on the corner of Church St and Kingsbury St has sections of 17/18th century wall, as well as internal 15th century stonework.

Turn left into Ivy Walk, an old passageway, where you will immediately see an iron cover mounted into the wall on your right, bearing the inscription 'E W Maundrell, Calne Wilts'. As you come out from under the arch turn around to look up at it. The 1870s stonework bears the name of Kerry Crescent, named after the Earl of Kerry, and has decorative stonework and a coat of arms.

The elaborate carvings over the arch at Ivy Walk (with the inscription 'Kerry Crescent')

Calne Heritage Centre, opened in 1905 as a public library.

Turn right and walk to the Calne Heritage Centre, the last stop on this walk – and a fitting one. This was originally a library and two inscriptions on the outside tell of how the building was gifted by Andrew Carnegie and that, 'This stone was laid July 16 1904 by the Earl of Kerry'. The library was opened in March 1905 and Calne's armorial bearings can still be seen above the doorway along with 'Public Library'. The former library became Calne Heritage Centre in October 2004, declared open by the current Earl of Kerry (see the plaque in the lobby). The centre is a marvellous resource for studying Calne's history; it hosts exhibitions and heritage events, and houses an archive library, along with Calne memorabilia and books for sale.

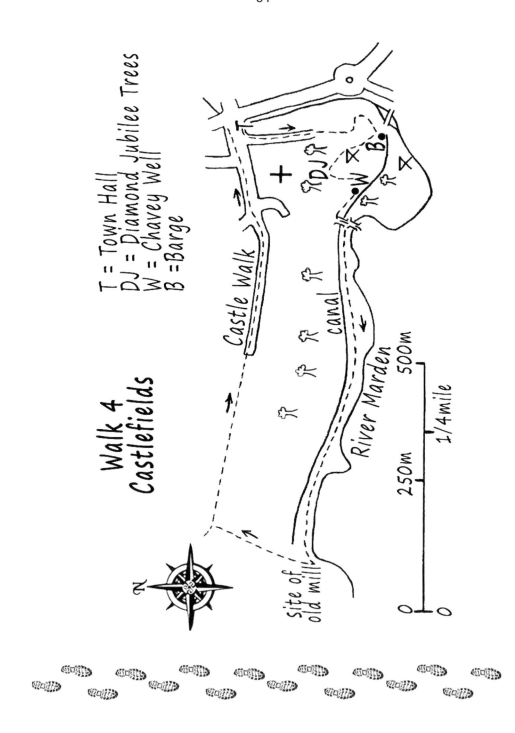

Walk 4
Castlefields

T = Town Hall
DJ = Diamond Jubilee Trees
W = Chavey Well
B = Barge

Castle Walk

canal

River Marden

site of
old mill

0   250m   500m

0   1/4 mile

Walk 4.
Castlefields

Summary of Walk 4

Distance: 2km (1¼ miles).
Circular or linear: circular.
Start point: Town hall, Calne.
End point: Lansdowne Strand Hotel.
Degree of difficulty: easy walking - pavements, gravel and grass.
Seasonal/weather restrictions: none.
Boots/wellies required: casual walking footwear recommended.
Public transport back to start point: not applicable.
Wheelchair accessible: only through Castlefields Park.
Refreshments and toilets: several cafés and pubs locally, and WC.
OS Explorer Map: 156.

This walk takes in Castlefields Park, one of Calne's recreational highlights with its river and canal walks, and includes the results of some fine

conservation and recreational projects. Many of these were driven by Castlefields Canal and River Park Association (CARP), founded in 1998, and who have since produced a Park Trail.

We begin at the Town

One of the mosaics designed by local children in the *Pocket Garden* at Castlefields Park.

Hall. Go around the back of the building and walk south along Patford St, passing under the modern arch until black iron gates are reached (image above), which mark the entrance to Castlefields Park. Posts next to the gate are each capped with a castle, symbolic of the one that may have stood on the adjacent hill. The gate itself incorporates a narrow boat/barge design, representing the canal which runs through the park. Wavy lines below symbolise both the canal and the waters of the River Marden, which flows through the park. The park was formerly the grounds of Castle House.

The narrow boat and lock gates at Castlefields Park. Canal artefacts are set into the ground (lower right).

After passing through gates, take the first path on the left, which leads to the 'Pocket Garden'. Sculpted bricks on the right were designed by pupils of Priestley School in Calne. A compass set into the ground contains the latitude and longitude of the locality, and celebrates ten years of

Some of the canal fittings recovered during restoration of the canal, now set into the ground next to the restored lock gates.

CARP. Continue on through the garden where more bricks, the result of the efforts of Calne Scouts, will be seen by a bench, with mosaics on a nature theme behind. Continue through a reedy area, until you come to more engraved bricks, designed by the Guides, as well as ceramic tiles set into ground.

From here take the short walk to the barge, or narrow boat, and the reconstructed lock, which was completed in 2012 (see above and Colour Plate 5). The installation was unveiled in May of that year and is the result of the fine efforts of CARP. It celebrates the Wilts and Berks Canal, a branch line of which served the town from 1802 to 1901, and terminated at The Wharf. The Calne branch was some three miles long and had three locks, and the narrow boats carried up to 20 tons of cargo, much of which served the Harris factory. The River Marden runs close to the canal here, and there were five mills downstream from where you now stand; its waters in fact fed the canal. The waters of the renovated canal can be seen beyond the narrow boat, and the reconstructed lock gates are on the site of the Town Lock (see image p. 13).

Nearby, some of the original canal memorabilia found locally are set into the ground (image above). A notice board on the narrow boat, and another nearby, tell the story of the history of the canal and of CARP's restoration projects. Yet another board to the south shows the route of the Fitness Trail, which was opened in 2005.

Now walk to the small tree standing within iron railings where paths meet. It is surrounded by ceramic tiles with music, arts and nature scenes. One tile informs us that the images commemorate thirty years of Calne's Music and Arts Festival; another celebrates Calne Choral Society. Note the nearby brasses mounted on short wooden posts; these are part of a nature trail and others can be found around the park. The images are in relief and can be rubbed to lift the designs onto paper. From here ascend the path behind the

Chavey Well at Castlefields, a source of pure water in the past, as it is today.

notice boards beyond the tree, passing the plaque celebrating the Fields In Trust Project of Queen Elizabeth's Diamond Jubilee of 2012.

At the top of the slopes you reach the summit of Castle Hill, said to be the site of an ancient fortified enclosure, and possibly a Saxon hall. In front of you is a plaque at ground level which celebrates the planting of the Jubilee Scots Pines. The inner circle was planted in 1897 for Queen Victoria's Diamond Jubilee, whilst the outer ring of pines was planted to mark the current Queen's Diamond Jubilee in 2012. A triangle of memorial benches stands in the centre.

From here walk down the path at the far side, in the direction of the bridge that is visible in the distance below. This descends to the canal, where you turn right to reach Chavey Well (or Chaveywell). This natural spring is one of several that issue from the hill, and its pure waters are refreshing to this day. There was once a pig farm here, no doubt benefiting from the springs. The site was restored by CARP in 2010 and a plaque (image p. 21) tells how the waters remained pure during typhoid epidemics of 1880 and 1890. Even today the steady flowing waters are cool and wonderful to drink, and are daily frequented by dogs and their walkers. Two stone pig heads mounted on the wall were once corbels at the Harris pork factory. Recently the Calne Environmental Network has planted wildflowers around

Chaveywell Bridge, which spans the old canal. The canal and the bridge were recently restored and a plaque celebrates the restoration.

the well, which add colour, and nectar for the bees, during summer months. Turning your back on the well, you can see that the water flows into the canal, although originally it would have fed the River Marden. The Wilts and Berks Canal Trust restored the canal and the bridge here. A rule of the canal stated, 'No boat shall be navigated upon any part of this canal with the stern foremost (except in passing to the nearest turning place)'. The penalty for breaking the decree was a fine of not less than 20 shillings (£1.00). Now go past the small wharf and cross Chaveywell Bridge, noting the plaque on its east side, which marks the re-opening of the wharf by the

Earl of Shelburne on 11th June, 1989. Once over the bridge, immediately turn left, where you will find a brass plaque (mounted on a low wooden post) which is engraved with plants such as teasels, which can be rubbed. In front of you is a 'hay meadow', as well as some apparatus of the Fitness Trail. From the plaque retrace your steps back along the path and bear left, passing under the arch to see the National Cycle Network signpost, which marks route no. 403; this route passes through Calne and we will encounter it again on other walks.

Retrace your steps back under the arch and go through the kissing gate

immediately on the left, between the two bridges. Follow this path, which is sandwiched between the River Marden on the left, and the canal on the right. Look out for wildlife along this section, such as mice, Heron, Kingfishers, butter-flies, and bats at dusk. Buzzards are also frequently seen

The weir near the site of Moss's Mill, with the waters of the Marden rushing through.

and heard overhead. Note the overflow from the canal just before the stile, which can be a haven for frogs. Cross the stile and continue through the field following a rough path. Keep going until you encounter a weir, which was built in 1996 to control the level of the canal between Calne and the A4 once dredging is completed and the canal restored. A little further on (west) you will encounter some runs of old brickwork, which is all that remains of Moss's Mill (which is shown on older OS maps SE of Berhills

Farm — see images below). The mill belonged to the Lord of Studley Manor from the mid or later 17th century, and perhaps even earlier. Corn was ground in part of it in the early 18th century, and in 1761 it contained two flour mills, and probably continued that way into the early 19th century. Baptists used to meet at the mill until they had their own place of worship in Calne. It was rebuilt as a corn mill in the 1820s and operated until 1962, when it was destroyed by fire.

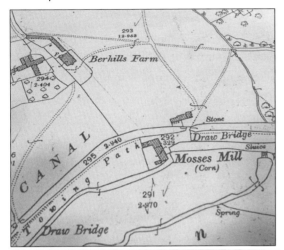

From the weir, head north towards the ridge, crossing a depression in the ground that marks the route of the canal and once the site of a draw bridge. Further west a tunnel was built to take the canal under the A4. The tunnel was around 92m (100 yards) long and was navigated by laying on the deck of the narrow boat and 'walking' along the roof of the tunnel. Horses were led over the road to meet the boat on the other side.

Walk up the slope, heading for the kissing gate visible in the distance. Go through the gate, turn right, and follow the path next to the hedgerow. After going through the next gate, you

Above: the area around Moss's Mill in 1899. Note the canal, with its draw bridges, towing path, the old weir, and the buildings of the mill. (From a copy in Calne Library.) Below: a photograph of outbuildings of Moss's Mill c.1900, showing lift bridge (person sitting on it).

will see a disused gate on the right, which once served the former orchard. Do not go through this gate, but rather continue straight on along the tarred path, known as Castle Walk, which passes behind houses.

Once the road begins, you will pass several interesting buildings. Castlefields House, on the left, is noticeable for the crenellated walls and parapets (resembling battlements). Built in the 1830s for Henry Merewether, then Town Clerk of the City of London, it is a picturesque Tudor Revival style build, with octagonal chimney stacks and a heraldic shield on the wall (image below). The Merewether family vault is in St Mary's (image p. 71). Old maps show that land north of the house (much of which is now Marden Court) was once the grounds of Castlefields House, laid out as lawn and copses, with a drive from a lodge on the A4, west of Calne Cemetery.

Next note the large, basin-like stone structure in front of the house, next to the lane. We have been informed by staff at Calne Heritage Centre that it is probably an old water trough for horses (image p. 63). Opposite the entrance to Castlefields House, the dwelling with the pillars (no. 22) was

Castlefields House, built in the 1830's for the Town Clerk of London.
Inset: heraldic coat of arms on the side of the house.

once the coach house and stables for the Castlefields House. Did the trough come from there perhaps? Other houses nearby are the Old surgery and the Old Dairy. Further on is the Baptist Church and Castle House, which we visited on other walks (see p. 21 and p. 45); old runs of wall can be seen at both properties, and there is a blue plaque at the entrance of Castle House (p. 20-1). From here go down Cox's Hill, where the Lansdowne Strand Hotel marks the end of this walk. Note the arch which once received horse drawn coaches during Calne's heyday as a coach stop on the London to Bath road. This establishment is well worth exploring for its historic features, both inside and out (see p. 45-47 for details).

This curious stone basin outside Castlefields House may have been a horse trough.

Walk 5
St Mary's Church and The Green

19

1

2

Kingsbury St 18

17

16

15

3

4 5 6

7

Horsebrook

The Green 8

14

13

9

12

10

11

N

0		125		250m
0		400		800ft

Walk 5.
St Mary's Church and The Green

Summary of Walk 5

Distance: 900m (approx. ½ mile).
Circular or linear: circular.
Start and end point: St Mary's Church, Calne.
Degree of difficulty: easy walking - pavements.
Restrictions: St Mary's open on Weds and Fri afternoons.
Boots/wellies required: no.
Public transport back to start point: not applicable.
Wheelchair accessible: small detour needed at Proclamation Steps at the end.
Refreshments and toilets: several cafés, pubs and toilets locally.
OS Explorer Map: 156 and 157.

Although we have already visited The Green briefly in Walk 1, we felt that it warranted its own walk, such is the historical interest here. It also made sense to include St. Mary's Church in this walk, for it is not only adjacent to The Green, but is in fact a fine, Grade I listed building and requires covering in some detail.

First stop is St. Mary's. There was certainly an early Saxon church here when the estate belonged to the Crown from the 9th or 10th century. The church standing in 1066 was probably on the site of the present church, although nothing of this is known to have survived. The earliest parts do date from Norman times, including the arches of the nave, part of the transept and the north wall. By AD 1155 it had attained its current size, sometimes being referred to as North Wiltshire's cathedral, and is still the largest church in the area. St Edmund was the vicar here when he was appointed Archbishop of Canterbury in 1234. He was known for his piety and work for the poor; the chapel on the south side is dedicated to St Edmund and contains late 14th century stonework.

The size of the church is testament to Calne's importance and wealth in medieval times. It was rebuilt by the generous donations of rich clothiers and wool merchants in the 15th century and is among a minority of medieval churches which are Grade I listed. From humble beginnings it was transformed outwardly into a Gothic building. The church once had a

St. Mary's Calne, once known as the 'Cathedral of North Wiltshire', because of its size and grandeur.

steeple, and then later a tower, the latter of which collapsed due to poor maintenance during a storm in Sept 1638, damaging much of the chancel in the process. The present tower was built c.1650, designed by Inigo Jones, and is said to be one of the few surviving examples by him in the Perpendicular/Gothic style. There were two further restorations in the 19th century; the four pinnacles capping the tower were once adorned with weather vanes, later removed after WW1 for safety reasons.

Before going inside the church, walk around to the south side, to examine the war memorial in the SW corner of the churchyard. On the west side of the south porch you will see decorative stonework that has been re-set into the wall. These are three panels from the grand chest tomb of Inverto Boswell, King of the Gypsies, who died of smallpox in Calne in 1774. The tomb in the churchyard formerly had a canopy, as the old illustration below shows. The rearing horse can be seen in both images. The original tomb had elaborate stonework, such as cherubs, Tuscan columns, skull and crossbones, and a scroll frieze. The monument was pulled down following protests from local parishioners after large gatherings of gypsies periodically, 'descended on the tomb to pay their respects'.

Now look through the iron gates of the south porch. On the ground beyond

Left: an old drawing of the canopied chest tomb of the 'King of the Gypsies', formerly in the churchyard. Right: the panels from the tomb now mounted on the south porch.

is an actual section of floor, in the form of a cross, from Stanley Abbey, the Cistercian foundation which once flourished just west of Calne (see images p. 68 and Walk 7). Equally interesting are the two coffin lids on either side, which have been mounted on the walls. They are both solid and carved, and are also from the abbey, presumably used to inter those of high status, possibly two abbots. These three relics, along with Spye Arch, are the finest surviving artefacts from the medieval abbey in Calne, although some smaller finds and stonework are in Chippenham Museum.

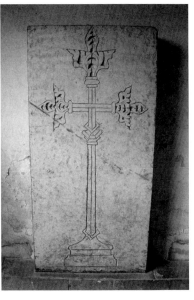

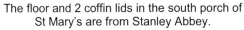

The floor and 2 coffin lids in the south porch of St Mary's are from Stanley Abbey.

Return to the other side of the church and enter through the north porch. On the way through note the fine memorial to the Merewether family on the right, telling of the exploits of various family members between 1837 and 1957. This family owned Castlefields House in Calne (see p. 62 for details). Above your head note the fan vaulting, which dates from the 15th century.

On entering the church note the solid Norman columns and arches, which date from the 12th century. The corbels above depict bishops and are 13th century. We will walk clockwise around the church, so turn left and follow the

The fine 16th century 'Parish Chest', which is mounted on a solid trunk of oak.

aisle that runs alongside the wall. You may notice on the floor a corbel of a pig's head, which once decorated the Harris factory, similar to the ones at Chavey Well (p. 58). Further on you will come to a large wooden chest. This is known as the 'Parish Chest', and is dated 1579. It was made during the reign of Elizabeth I and the lid bears her insignia. The chest is iron-bound, and has three strong locks dated 1603. The chest is wonderfully, almost surreally, embedded in a trunk of solid oak!

The Victorian pulpit and grand organ.

Turn left into the north transept and you see the beautiful war memorial window, designed by Christopher Wall in 1921. In vibrant colours, it features St Michael vanquishing a dragon (see Colour Plate 1). Next take a look at the fine organ. A plaque tells how it was gifted by the Harris family in 1908. The 19th century Victorian wooden pulpit in front of the organ features the disciples, intricately carved, and was gifted by Rev Duncan's wife. Note the small dragon emerging from the chalice held by John the Divine. Next to the altar is a finely carved bench end featuring Madonna and Child.

Walking around to face the altar, one is struck by the magnificence of the reredos behind, made of Corsham freestone in 1901 (Colour Plate 6). Golden and intricately carved it features Saxon saints, bishops and three scenes featuring Jesus. In the centre is the Crucifixion, which portrays Mary

Magdalene (whom many think was Jesus' wife) weeping at his feet. To the top left of the reredos is St Dunstan, famously associated with Calne for his 'miracle' (which we spoke of on p. 7). He is holding a pair of tongs; it is said that later in his life, whilst living in his hermitage at Glastonbury Abbey, the Devil came to tempt him but the saint seized him by the head with a pair of tongs to subdue him.

The reredos behind the altar is multi-coloured and beautifully carved (also see Colour Plate 6).

Mary Magdalene also appears either side of the altar in two other windows. On the left an angel is announcing the resurrection to Mary, and on the right Jesus appears to her after he has risen. Continue around to the south part of the chancel, where on the wall is another memorial to the Merewether family. The windows here are dated 1847 and 1851, and portray more biblical scenes.

Moving further around into the south transept, one is greeted by a very dark painting, literally! It was painted by an Italian artist and depicts St Peter preaching in the catacombs. The best views of it are from close-up on either side. In front of the painting is a brass cross on the floor, which seems tailor made for brass-rubbing.

Further on around you will come into St Edmund's Chapel. Edmund was the vicar of Calne from 1222 until his appointment as Archbishop of Cant-

terbury in 1234, a position he held until 1240. Fine golden sculptures behind the altar show the three wise men visiting the newborn Christ. To the left of the altar is a memorial to Dr Jan Ingen Housz (1730-1799), the Dutch scientist, whose blue plaque we visited on Walk 1 (see p. 24). This memorial was erected in 1995 by admirers and relatives from both the UK and the Netherlands. Next to the altar is also a 15th century piscina. Corbels above your head show Kings and Queens, whilst at the other end of the chapel is a tapestry showing St Edmund himself (image left).

The door of the south porch is usually locked but may be opened on request when the church is manned by volunteers on Wednesday and Friday afternoons. Mike Rawle is one such volunteer who is a mine of information.

Left: bell dated 1658. Right: the plaque above the Merewether family vault.

In the south aisle of nave you can view an almost complete roll of St Mary's vicars going back to Norman times.

Nearby is a huge bell, dated 1658, which was once the no. 3 bell, replaced by a new one in 1928 which was paid for by the 6th Lord Lansdowne, in honour of his father. Close by is the 15th century font, which is not in its original position, with a modern cover. Overlooking it is the west window, dedicated to the Hungerford family and dated 1867. Walking a little way east from the font is a brass plaque set into the floor, informing us that the Merewether family vault lies beneath. The kitchen area used to be the baptistry and has two windows depicting aspects of Jesus' life.

Mike Rawle kindly gave us a tour of the tower, which is not for the fainthearted! We viewed the workings of the clock, which was made in 1848 by Dents of London, the same company responsible for the clock in the tower of Big Ben. One of St Mary's bells, called the Sanctum Bell, is in fact pre-Reformation and is dedicated to St. Andrew. The roof affords

The view south from the top of the tower of St. Mary's, looking towards The Green. The almshouses can be seen in the foreground.

breathtaking vistas of Calne and the landscape beyond, such as the Cherhill White Horse, the Bowood Estate, High Penn and Morgan's Hill. Below us was a fine view of The Green, which is, fittingly, our next destination.

Once outside the church, turn left and exit the churchyard via the west gate, which exits into Church Street. Turn left and you will come to the junction with Kingsbury St. Here you will pass the War Memorial (stop 2 on this walk's map) with its sword set into the shaft, which we also passed in Walk 1. Turn left into Kingsbury St, keeping to the left hand side of the road until you come to The Green. There are so many listed buildings in this part of old Calne, that we are sticking to the historical highlights of The Green, at least as we see them.

Weaver's House on The Green.

Stop 3 is The Weaver's House, complete with its own blue plaque, informing us that the building was once a 'wool trade workshop'. It was probably built in the late 18th century to house machinery for the spinning and carding of wool into yarn, when such machinery was still horse driven. The original archway can still be seen, and in its heyday skilled Flemish weavers were employed in Calne. Weaver's House was later used by Harris's as a sawdust store, known then as Sawdust House.

Further along, the buildings set back were once an orphanage (as shown on 1899 maps), and during WWI were used to billet soldiers. Later it was a building for women working at Harris's, and later still was a school.

Stops 4, 5 and 6 are nos. 10, 12, and 13 The Green. These well illustrate the architecture related to the medieval wool industry, and reflect the wealth and high status of their occupants; they were re-fronted in the 18th century. No 10 was the residence of the Bailey family, who were wealthy clothiers, and until recently was the home of Peter Treloar, whose books of old photos of Calne are legendary, and were much appreciated during our research for this book. He was a borough councillor for 25 years and former Mayor. He was at the forefront of the Marden House renovation project, and also had a close association with Calne Methodist Church. Originally a Cornishman, he was an ardent railway enthusiast, and at the age of 70 received an MBE from the Queen. Sadly, he passed away in 2013.

House no. 13 shows some older oak beams of an earlier frontage behind the downstairs windows, partially obscuring them. Architect Robert Adam resided here whilst working at Bowood House. The building is also notable for its 'pineapple' finials, a sure sign of opulence. Behind these buildings are long gardens down to the river, where cloth was hung out to dry.

Continue along to Horsebrook, passing Maundrell House, to stop 7, which is the open space at Edred's Court (named after the Saxon king), and once Maundrell's Yard. The modernized Victorian buildings on the right are of the

The former Technical School in The Green.

former iron foundry, where from 1885 Edward W Maundrell produced a variety of ironwork and equipment, including machinery for the Harris factory, agricultural implements and cheese pressers. Some local drain covers still bear the Maundrell name (image p. 83).

Retrace your steps to The Green and pause at the SE corner, stop 8. The Green was long known as Kingsbury Green, as shown on the 1899 OS map. This area was perhaps the earliest place of residence in Calne, probably from Saxon times. Many of the buildings you see around The Green are listed, most having been refaced in the 18th and 19th centuries. Fairs were often held on the Green – including a travelling zoo with elephants in the 1920s! Bonfires were also a regular attraction, such as those celebrating the Silver Jubilee of 1935 and the Coronation in 1937. A Green Fair and May Day celebrations, complete with a May Pole bedecked with colourful ribbons, were also held here. A photo from around 1900 shows donkeys grazing at The Green; they were often used to transport sand and other goods around the area.

Now cross back to the house which bears the date of 1894 over the door – stop 9 (image previous page). On the 1899 map the building is shown as the 'Technical School'.

After the gap, the next building is Priestley House (stop 10). This dates, along with no. 20, from the 16th century, although only cellars and an ornate spiral staircase have survived from that date. They were rebuilt in mid-17th century and later refaced in 1758, a date shown high above the door. Dr Joseph Priestley famously stayed here from 1772 to 1779 (as a notice on the door testifies), whilst working in his laboratory at Bowood

House, under the patronage of the Marquis of Lansdowne. Note the boot scrapers that are adorned with Griffins outside no. 20.

Continue along the pavement, passing the 1935 Grade II listed telephone box of a previous walk (see page 51).

Priestley House, where the doctor lived in the 18th century, whilst researching in his laboratory at Bowood.

The old stables at the side of the White Hart, and the antlered beast himself.

On the corner is stop 11, the White Hart, a former coaching inn, as the arch and double gates testify. The inn is recorded in 1659, although some of the building is thought to date from the 16th century. A pre-WWI advert featuring the White Hart boasted 'good stabling' and 'B&B from 4 shillings'! There is a fine portico with steps and columns. On the east side you can see the antlered hart (or is it a cow?), whose antlers were recently reinstated after many years absence. The out-buildings at the side of the pub are late-18th and early 19th century, and are said to be excellent and well preserved examples of coaching inn stables.

The inscription 'Boys' School 1829' on the crenellated tower of the former school.

From here you can see the former King George pub (now a private residence) on the corner of Church Street, and, on the opposite corner, a drinking fountain, stop 12 (image p. 51). Behind the fountain is stop 13, which is the former Boys' School (image above). It was founded in 1557 by Walter Fynamore. The date of 1829 on the side of the building testifies to a later rebuild in the Tudor Revival Style. Note the cherub in the alcove and the crenellated tower and turrets. Old photographs show a Crimean War cannon in the garden behind the fountain. This was melted down for the war effort during World War II.

Continuing along the west side of The Green we soon come to no. 23A, which is stop 14. This was another school, this time for girls, opened soon after the boy's school. Above the arched window is a statue of a female figure.

Walk further on until you come to stop 15, the building that is set back, which was the original Bentley School, founded as a grammar school in 1660 by John Bentley of Richmond, Surrey. Some remains of the original schoolhouse can be seen in the lower walls at the rear, in Church Street. The front of the building appears to bear the date of 1905. It was used by

House nos. 30 -30B was the original site of the famous St Mary's Girls' School, founded in 1872.

Wiltshire Council for a time and is now a private residence.

Continue to the corner, to house nos. 30, 30A and 30B – stop 16. This was formerly a 16th century building, and later was the original site of Calne's now famous public school, St. Mary's Girls. The school was founded in 1872 by vicar John Duncan and Elinor

Gabriel. It was later moved to Lansdowne Villa, and then to its present site in Curzon Street in 1908. Around the corner walk until you reach no. 32, where you will see an old arch, formerly for the receiving of horses and coaches in times gone by (stop 17).

You will now come to the famous Dr Tounson's Almshouses (stop 18), one of the oldest buildings in Calne. These curious old buildings were commissioned after the Civil War by Dr Tounson, vicar of Bremhill and son of the Bishop of Salisbury, for the housing of elderly widows of the parish. He had lost his livelihood during the war but was later reinstated by Charles II, and gifted the almshouses to the poor of Calne in gratitude. There were originally eight dwellings in this listed building, but now it is divided into just four, accessed through very low doors! The original plaque still graces the front of the building (see image p. 25). The curved sweep of the building is notable, a feature well seen from the top of the church tower (image p. 72).

From here cross the road and walk down the passage opposite, which skirts the side of the churchyard. You may be lucky to see the peregrine falcons that have made the tower of St. Mary's their vantage point from which to hunt. The numerous finds of bird carcasses at the foot of the tower bear

The Tounson Almshouses in Kingsbury Street date from 1682,
as the original plaque testifies.

witness to their success rate.

At the end of the passage, just before you descend the steps, note the drain cover, which bears the 'Maundrell Calne' inscription, although rather worn; we shall see a better example on the next walk. Now go down Proclamation Steps (stop 19), to find an attendant rectangular blue plaque on the wall of Proclamation House (images p. 25 and below). This was installed in 1977 in honour of the Queen's Silver Jubilee, and the inscription tells us that, 'from time immemorial' Royal Proclamations and other important announcements were read out from the steps. This walk back through time ends here in Mill Street.

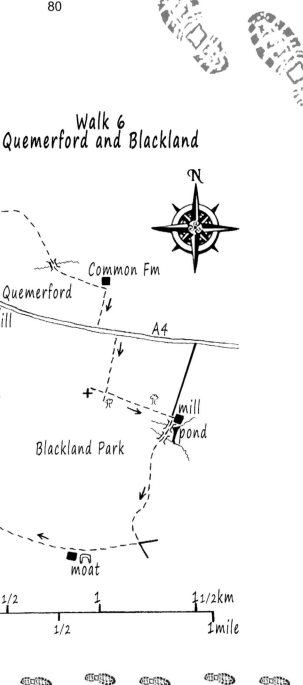

Walk 6
Quemerford and Blackland

Calne

The Green

mill

R Marden

PH

Quemerford

Common Fm

mill

A4

Motor Museum

shop

Blackland Park

mill pond

moat

N

0		1/2		1		1 1/2km

0			1/2			1mile

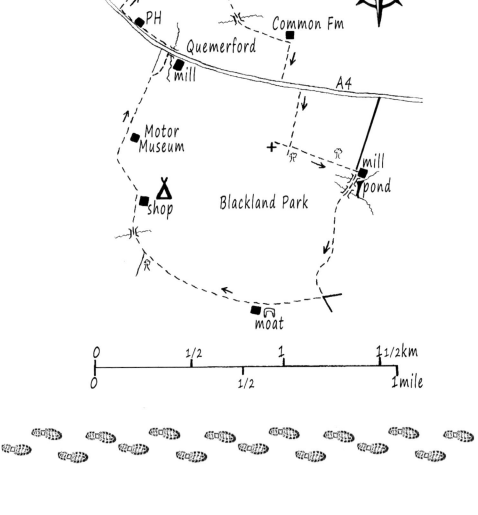

Walk 6.
Quemerford and Blackland

Summary of Walk 6

Distance: 7.5km (approx. 4½ miles).
Circular or linear: circular.
Start point and end point: The Green, Calne.
Degree of difficulty: easy walking, some open fields; no steep slopes.
Restrictions: Some muddy tracks in winter; Motor Museum is seasonal.
Boots/wellies required: stout footwear recommended. Wellies in some parts following wet winter weather.
Public transport back to start point: not applicable.
Recommendation: Sunday, when traffic is lighter at Blackland.
Wheelchair accessible: mostly unsuitable for wheelchairs.
Refreshments & toilets: shop/toilets at caravan site; Talbot Inn near end.
OS Explorer Map: 157.

This walk takes us across the eastern side of Calne, through Quemerford and Blackland, combining quiet riverside walks, country lanes, as well as industrial heritage, including two surviving mills.

From the south-east corner of The Green, we set off down Horsebrook. Beyond Maundrell House, the open space at Edred's Court (named after the Saxon king) was once the yard of Maundrell's. The modernized Victorian buildings on the right are from the former iron foundry, from where Edward W Maundrell produced a variety of ironwork and equipment. The iron foundry and engineering works was built here in the late 1850s, originally managed by George Gough. In 1885 Edward Maundrell took over the business; he had previously made bicycles and had an engineering business in a former nonconformist chapel in Back Road. Maundrell's made a wide range of goods, including railings, drain and manhole covers (see below), lamp posts, and in the 1920s grew as a manufacturer of equipment for the Harris pork factory. In the mid 20th century Maundrell Foundries continued as iron founders and engineers and c.1952 employed around 30 people. However, the foundry was closed in 1957, although the site continued to be used for engineering until the 1990s.

Continuing down the lane, note the old raised pavement on the south side. Further on, where houses now stand on the left, there used to be a gas works. Cross over the river to Horsebrook (or Swaddon's) Mill, the two story building in front of you, which still has a sluice at the rear. The mill was conveyed by a clothier Thomas Swaddon in 1713, when it incorporated a grist mill and two fulling mills, and later by Mary Swaddon in 1726. It stood between Lows Mill and Kew Lane Mill and was later became known as Horsebrook Mill. Corn was being ground there in 1772, but apparently not by the 19th century.

Horsebrook or Swaddon's Mill. The site was a mill from the 1700s, and was rebuilt in 1822.

From 1807, when Mr Daniel Bailey became tenant, the mill may have been wholly a cloth mill. In 1822 it was rebuilt as a nine-bayed and five-storey cloth mill with mullioned windows and two breast-shot wheels. From then until 1849 Joseph Bailey & Co. (formerly George Bailey & Co.) traded as clothiers from Horsebrook mill and premises at The Green. There was a weaving shop near the mill in 1828 and was probably there until the late 1840s. From 1849 to 1871 flax was processed at Horsebrook Mill by T. L. Henly; the mill was unfortunately damaged by fire in 1861, but was still operational in 1871, recorded as being driven by both water and steam. The mill had probably gone out of use by 1885, although the waterwheel survived as late as 2001.

Go around the left side of the building into Anchor Road. Next to it, at the foot of an embankment, look for one of Maundrell's drain covers (image left), made locally just up the lane. Several others can be seen around Calne (such as the one near Proclamation Steps on the previous walk).

From here retrace your steps, passing the mill, until you reach the bridge, and take the well-defined, signposted public footpath east, which follows the south side of the Marden. Further along, just before the path ascends a flight of steps to the road, note the island and mill race at the site of a former mill. At the top of the steps turn left and go down Brewers Lane (once called Cow Lane) to the bridge. Note Watersmeet Cottage, on an island, the site of Kew's Mill, and look over the east side of the bridge for old structures beneath. From here continue east along the pleasant riverside footpath. Further along, a sluice gate can be seen in the river, and beyond this the waters suddenly, and surprisingly, become wider and more languid.

On reaching the road, turn left and cross the metal footbridge that spans the river at a tranquil spot. Crossing the stile on the far side, turn right and follow the path. Ignore the stile on the right at a sunken hollow (which can be muddy in winter), and carry straight on. Ignore the entrance to another field on the right, instead keeping straight ahead with the hedge on your right. Cross the next stile, ignoring the bridge to your right which spans River's Brook, a tributary of the Marden which flows from Cherhill, and continue straight ahead along the public right of way, and through a gate into a large field. The landscape opens up, and the Cherhill White Horse and the Lansdowne Monument demand attention in the distance.

Turn right and follow the south edge of the field, until a gap in hedge takes the public footpath over River's Brook, by now just a trickle. Turn left and walk towards the buildings of Common Farm (walking in the general

direction of the Lansdowne Monument). Head for a gap in the hedge just south of the buildings, and cross over the stile. Turn right and follow the tarmac drive, with its poplar avenue, to the A4, passing the resident alpacas!

At the busy main road, turn left and then after about 100m cross the

The Cherhill White Horse and the Lansdowne Monument seen from fields north of Quemerford.

road when you see signs for St Peter's Church. Go down the bridleway to the church car park, noting the fine views of the Cherhill White Horse, the monument, and Morgan's Hill (marked by masts). We have now entered Blackland Park. In the 10th century, or perhaps earlier, the land, which was to become a parish, belonged to the King's estate of Calne, as part of Calstone (possibly 'Calne's east tun') called the 'Black Land of Calston'. By the late 12th century Blackland had separated from Calstone, and by this time its church and probably a manor house had already been built. In 1194 the manor, church, a farmstead, and a mill had all adopted the name Blackland. The Quakers are recorded at Blackland in the 17th–18th century, and Blackland Park played host to Girl Guide rallies in the 1930s.

Follow the signposted path to the church. St Peter's stands midst an atmospheric setting, surrounded by large yews and tall redwood sequoias. The church is usually locked but keys may be obtained (tel: 01249 816522). In the porch is a memorial to one of the Hungerford family dated 1675, and next to it a list of rectors going back to 1583. On entering the church, one is struck by how dark it is; the altar end is the least illuminated we have ever seen, small windows and large trees conspiring to block out much of the daylight; despite this, the atmosphere is wonderful. The main focus behind the altar is a scene of the Crucifixion, portraying Mary

St Peter's at Blackland. This small isolated church is concealed in Blackland Park.

Magdalene grieving at the foot of the cross. In modern times, the church suffered a roof fire, in January 1940, during WWII. The squire's 18th century mansion can be seen nearby.

This little church stands on an alignment of sacred sites that comprise the Wessex Astrum, a huge landscape hexagram that includes Glastonbury, Avebury and Stonehenge (Knight & Perrott, 2008). From here the line goes through the Cherhill White Horse and on to Avebury.

Retrace your steps back to the car park and take the public foot path straight ahead, walking to the far end of the large field, towards the old mill in the distance. At the far end cross the stile and pass through the small copse to the road. Turn right, taking care to follow the grass verge, and soon Blackland Mill is reached on the other side of road.

Blackland Mill (images below and Colour Plate 7) is probably on the site of a 13th century mill and historically always seems to have been used for corn. It was rebuilt c.1800 to include a new mill house and detached granary. Milling temporarily ceased between 1915 and 1920 but thereafter

Blackland Mill. Left: A photograph from 1903 showing the mill owner, his family and workers loading grain. Right: the mill today, showing the surviving waterwheel.

continued until 1982, when the mill was restored. From 1983 to 1993 wholemeal flour was still produced here until milling finally ceased, making it one of the last mills in the area to close after some 800 years of use. Unusually, the waterwheel is still in situ, and periodically rotates due to water action, particularly after heavy rain. Passing the mill one can stand on the second bridge and view the waterfall that cascades over the old sluice behind the mill.

Continue south along the road, staying on the grass verge (this road can be busy from Monday to Friday with lorries going to and from the landfill and recycling centre). Fine views are offered east to Morgan's Hill, with the village of Calstone nestling beneath. Cross over at the double bend, and turn right into the road signposted 'Stockley and Heddington'. Approaching Blackland Farm, over the hedge you will get glimpses of water that still fills a late Medieval Moat (the dead tree and platform are on the former island that was enclosed by the moat). As early as the 13th century, Blackland Farm existed on a defensive moated site, a rectangle on which stood the farm, said to be as grand as Blackland Manor House itself. Some of the present buildings date from the 16th century.

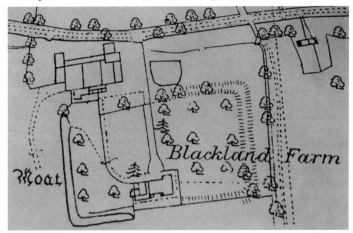

19th century map of Blackland Farm, showing the rectangular form of the medieval moat.

Continue along the lane, turning right at the road junction (signposted to Calne and Caravan Park). The caravan, camping and leisure centre offers a small shop (in reception) and a toilet block for patrons. The road continues north into a housing estate. Eventually, take the path on the right, which follows a stream between the entrances to The Croft and Rivermead. This path affords good views of Lower Quemerford Mill (image below), its fine chimney and two waterfalls surviving as impressive remnants of the mill, now converted to dwellings. Turn right at the main road and stand on the bridge over the River Marden, where you get a fine view of the chimney (which served a 14 horsepower engine) and both waterfalls. Further along you will soon encounter the main gate of the mill, with the large delivery yard beyond. Quemerford was almost certainly part of the King's estate that was granted to others from the late 12th century. It was a largely

Lower Quemerford Mill, which still has its chimney, sluice waterfalls and other features.

agricultural area with no early nucleated settlement. There was a fulling mill locally by 1550, and two by 1646, when the Chivers family were prominent locally; later still a third mill was built. Around 1800 the Lower Mill was rebuilt as a water-powered cloth factory. The engine was added in 1815, and by 1841 had been converted to a grain grinding mill when the cloth industry failed. It continued producing animal food-stuffs. During the 1850-70s paper was made at Quemerford.

Retrace your steps over the bridge and now head west along the main road towards Calne. Cross over and walk along the raised pavement, passing Wessington Park (once the site of the council swimming baths, built in 1896, which was fed by river water, and operated until around 1939). Locally a business called Blackford's made steam cranes in the 1920s.

On the front of no. 17 is a curiosity in the form of a seemingly Dali-inspired sinuous grandfather clock! The face bears the inscription, 'Knightsbridge Station London 1852' (image below).

The bendy grandfather clock at house no. 17.

Continue past the Talbot Inn (food available), passing Wessington Court and the school, outside of which is a newly installed street map of Calne. At the far end of school take the alleyway that passes alongside the church. About 100m down this path is an entrance into the churchyard of the Church of the Holy Trinity. The church was built in 1852-3 (according to the faded inscription on the porch), in the Gothic Revival style, mainly at the expense of Canon John Guthrie on land donated by Lord Lansdowne. The new churchyard eased a predicament, as by that time St Mary's graveyard was full.

Continue down the alleyway, turning left at the road (ignore the bridge we crossed earlier), and when the road ends retrace your steps along the quiet riverside path we traversed at the start of the walk; this will return you to The Green.

Holy Trinity Church.

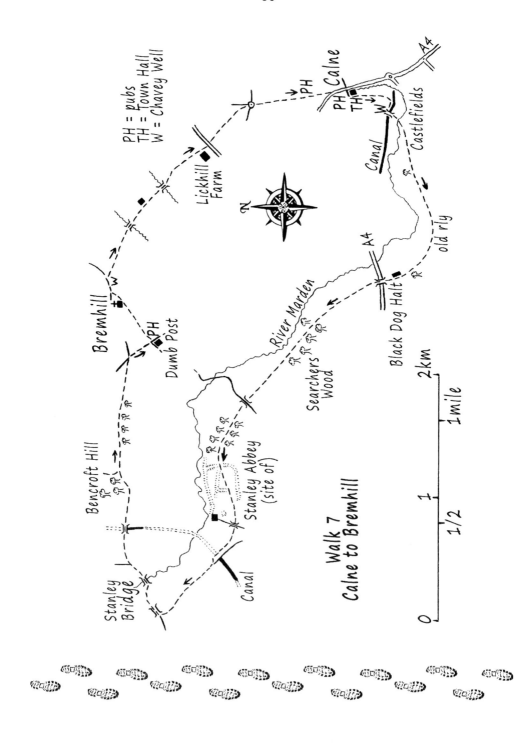

PH = pubs
TH = Town Hall
W = Chavey Well

Calne

A4

PH

PH
TH
W
Castlefields

Canal

old rly

Lickhill
Farm

N

Bremhill

PH
Dumb Post

Bencroft Hill

Stanley
Bridge

Canal

Stanley Abbey
(site of)

River Marden

A4

Searchers
Wood

Black Dog Halt

Walk 7
Calne to Bremhill

0   1/2   1   1 mile

2 km

Walk 7.
Calne to Bremhill

Summary of Walk 7

Distance: 11km (approx. 6¾ miles).
Circular or linear: circular.
Start point and end point: Town Hall, Calne.
Degree of difficulty: mainly easy walking; moderate hill up to Bremhill.
Restrictions: Dumb Post opening times; and sections of the old railway line cycle route may be closed on Thursdays 9am–3pm Nov-Feb, when shooting may be taking place on adjacent Bowood Estate.
Boots/wellies required: stout footwear.
Public transport back to start point: not applicable.
Wheelchair accessible: much is unsuitable for wheelchairs (several stiles and narrow footbridges).
Refreshments and toilets: The Dumb Post at Bremhill.
OS Explorer Map: 156.

This walk goes from Calne to the pleasant hilltop village of Bremhill via the old railway line, passing the site of Stanley Abbey, and returning through open fields, crossing two streams.

We begin at Calne Town Hall. Around the rear of the building go along Patford Street and through the iron gates into Castlefields Park, which we described in detail in Walk 4. At the narrow boat turn right and follow the canal path passing Chavey Well (images p. 21 & 58). The refreshing waters from this spring remained pure even during typhoid epidemics. From here cross Chaveywell Bridge (image p. 59), which was restored by the Wilts and Berks Canal Trust. Look for the plaque on the east side of the bridge. This path is signposted Cycle Route 403; go under the ironwork arch and you

will encounter a fine cycle route post. Inscriptions tell how it is one of 1000 such posts erected as part of the Millennium Project, marking the creation of the National Cycle Network. The graphics are a cross section through geological time, with trilobites near the base, fishes, ammonites and a dinosaur further up, with Man's industrial legacy at the top (see book cover image). The cycling distances to Bristol, Chippenham and Avebury are also given.

Follow the path west. Visible on the skyline to the south is the new housing estate that marks the site of the old railway station and sidings. Go through the gate by the embankment and over a stream, which feeds the River Marden below. This raised path is now following the course of the old railway line, which served Calne from 1863-1965. There are views to the north to Berhills Farm across the Marden flood plain. Just this side of a

1960s photograph of Black Dog Halt, shortly before the line was closed.

bridge over another tributary is an information board, showing CARP's 'Country Park Vision Plan' for the future of Castlefields. Views from here show how the course of old canal mirrors that of the River Marden.

Continue along the old railway track to the site of Black Dog Halt, which was opened in April 1905. Two stretches of platform survive plus the old station sign. The line was closed in 1965 and the station demolished shortly after; the track was taken up in 1967. The modern gate and railings have railway-related decoration, including a steam train chugging towards you (complete with puffing smoke) and two black dogs!

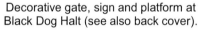
Decorative gate, sign and platform at Black Dog Halt (see also back cover).

From here continue over the steel footbridge, suspended from a bow string truss, which was built to span the A4 in 1999-2000. Cross the bridge, noting views in the east of the Cherhill White Horse and the Lansdowne Monument. Continue along the old railway path, which is now elevated. Before Searchers Wood note Conigre Farm on opposite side of the valley, and the Marden on this side of it, to which the canal ran adjacent along this stretch. There was once a mill here, New Mill, and two locks, called the Conigre or Conigie Locks, with an attendant Lock House. As you walk further note the hazel coppicing, and you will also cross an old railway bridge, with its large horizontal girders and huge rivets.

Next you will pass under a bridge that takes a road over the former railway track. Note the large blocks of local fossiliferous Corallian (Jurassic) limestone in the stones that comprise the bridge. Continue along the track through woodland, at the end of which is a gate, through which you will exit into more open ground. Along the next stretch note the numerous bumps, embankments and ditches which mark Stanley (or Stanleigh) Abbey, the medieval Cistercian monastery, and the only one of that order in Wiltshire. The path crosses moat-like ditches on two occasions. The Abbey was founded by the Empress Matilda in 1151 in Pewsham Forest and was given to the monks of Quarr Abbey, on the Isle of Wight. It was later moved

to Stanley in 1154 by Henry II. The Cistercians were an offshoot of the Benedictines, from whom the Knights Templar originated. They were well versed in sacred geometry and their buildings reflected this knowledge, often being placed on landscape alignments with other sacred sites.

The abbey here had a fulling mill as early as 1189, making it one of the earliest recorded. Most of the monastery was rebuilt in the early 13th century and eventually grew to a precinct of 24 acres. The influence of the Abbey grew; Abbot Nicholas entertained King John here in

Above: Cistercian monk.
Below: A section of Cistercian abbey wall, showing precise geometrical form and measure.

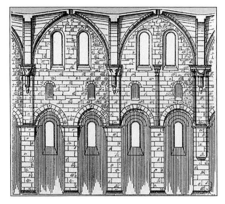

October 1200, and in 1210 Abbot Thomas attended a meeting of King John and the Cistercian abbots at York. In 1280 King Edward gave stone to the abbey for a chamber to be built for his personal use and according to the abbey chronicle he used it in the spring of 1282. Princess Mary, the Bishop of Salisbury, and Edward II, all stayed at the Stanley Abbey during the early years of the 14th century.

The site was excavated by Sir Harold Brakspear in 1905-6 and a plan made of the buildings and the 180ft long church to the south. The site is marked by the remains of mill/fish-ponds, enclosure ditches and the

A floor tile from the abbey showing fleur-de-lys, now in Chippenham Museum.

foundations of buildings, and finds of coffins, coins and encaustic tiles were recorded. When the railway was cut through the area, more burials were found, plus 'a blacksmith's forge with coal', and architectural debris built into farm walls. A 'font' or stoup from the church was found on the lawn of the new farmhouse in 1894. To the east was an infirmary hall and a circular dovecote to the north. The church incorporated 12th–14th century features, and cloisters that had been rebuilt in the 14th century. The Abbey was dissolved by Henry VIII in 1536, although a number of 15th century walls indicate a post-Reformation use of short duration. At the Dissolution the land passed into the possession of Sir Edward Baynton, who plundered the materials to build his manor house at Bromham.

A few artefacts have survived, such as tiles, a gable cap and other stonework, now in Chippenham museum. Two coffin lids and a fine section of floor from the abbey are in the south porch of St Mary's, Calne (see images p. 68), and Spye Arch (walk 9) is made from the entrance gate of the abbey. It is sad that all that remains now in situ of this once important abbey are a few bumps and ditches in these fields. It is believed that the site of the abbey water-mill is now occupied by Old Abbey Farm.

Further on is an old railway maintenance unit. Then you pass under the bridge that takes the road to Old Abbey Farm to the north, and a little further on pass through a gate, where there is a small car park. This is Studley Bridge and the place where the railway passed over the canal, and overgrown canal ditches can be seen either side. A few feet beyond the gate some brickwork from the canal bridge can be seen underfoot crossing the path. Immediately to the north was an aqueduct taking the canal over the Marden, but when this collapsed in 1901 the canal was abandoned.

Leaving the course of the railway, proceed to the road and note another Cycle Route signpost, telling us that it is 3 miles to Chippenham and 3¼ to Calne. Pass the sign and continue west along the road, following cycle route signs. The embankments of the former railway can be seen on the right, which passes through the back garden of Rose Cottage further on. You will go by the entrance to Stanley Mill, one of twenty that once operated in the Calne area. There were also two locks at Stanley.

Passing Pound Farm on the left, you will encounter another cycle route post (image above). It records the distance of 6 miles to Lacock and 2½ to

Chippenham. Go through the gate next to it and down the path to reach the last railway bridge we will encounter on this walk. It is slightly longer than the others and offers more of an echo! Here once stood Stanley Bridge Halt (image left), which was opened in April 1905.

Plate 2: Proclamation Steps and St Mary's (Walks 1 & 5).

Plate 1: War memorial window in St Mary's Church, Calne (Walk 5).

Plate 3: This fountain at the Rec once stood in the centre of Calne (Walk 2).

Plate 4: Hilmarton Church (Walk 13).

Plate 5 (above): narrow boat and reconstructed lock at Castlefields Park (Walk 4).
Plate 6 (below): the magnificent reredos at St Mary's Church, Calne (Walk 5).

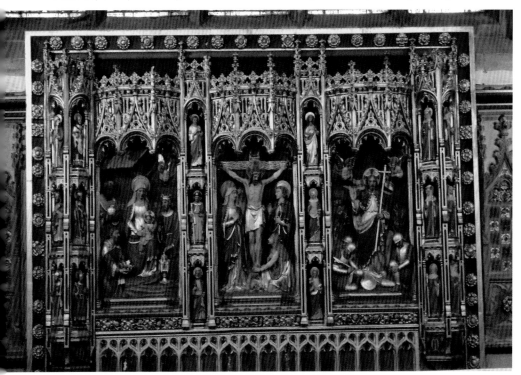

Plate 7 (above): Blackland Mill (Walk 6). Plate 8 (below): cottage, Compton Bassett (Walk 11).

Pl. 9 (above): Ivy Inn, Heddington (Walk 14). Pl. 10 (below): Cherhill White Horse (Walks 12 & 16).

Plate 11 (above): Kellaways Church (Walk 10). Plate 12 (below): Maud's Causeway (Walk 10).

Plate 13 (above): Drinker Moth caterpillar (2in/5cm long), and Orange Tip butterflies (Walk 15).
Plate 14 (below): Avebury, taken by Peter Knight during a flight (Walks 15 & 16).

Plate 15 (above): Silbury Hill, reflected in flood water (Walk 16).
Plate 16 (below): Equinox sunrise at West Kennet Long Barrow (Walk 16).

Retrace your steps to road and turn right, and right again at the junction (following directions to Bremhill, Stanley and Calne). On the top of the bridge you can look westwards along the course of the old railway, towards Chippenham in the distance.

You will soon come to Stanley Bridge, which crosses a fast flowing Marden, the capping stones of which are flat and low enough to afford a resting place. Further along at the fork take the road right, which gradually rises. You will pass the old Primitive Methodist Chapel and will soon cross the course of the old Wilts and Berks Canal, where white railings line the road; the course of the canal is marked to the south by the tree line. Continue on, ascending the hill, where Holly House, the cottage on the left near the top, is dated 1890, and has heraldry that includes a crown, a bundle of wheat and scythes (image right).

Near the top of the hill vistas open up, with fine views to Morgan's Hill (with its two masts), Cherhill White Horse and the Lansdowne Monument, and south to the spire of Derry Hill church. Continue up the lane, and after the double bend the road levels off, passing ornamented gardens and ponds. The bridleway that goes off to the left skirts the slopes of Bencroft Meadows SSSI, designated for its botanical diversity,

The Dumb Post Inn at Bremhill offers a welcome break on this walk.

which includes Thistles, Orchids and Dyers Green-Weed. At the junction turn right, and soon right again (signposted Ratford and Calne).

The Dumb Post Inn in Bremhill will soon be encountered (image above). This great rural pub offers good food, a children's playground, and glorious views from the terrace. This popular inn was once part of the Bowood Estate of the Earl of Shelburne, and it is thought that the inn got it's name from the custom of mailmen pinning letters on a post outside the inn for the locals, before the days of the Royal Mail. The mid-late 18th century inn is Grade II listed, and houses 200 year old documents, including a copy of the rules of the Dumb Post Friendly Society in 1770. This was a sick benefit or thrift club, and these old documents describe the Club Walk in Whit Week, a trek that proceeded from the inn to the village cross, with a service in St. Martin's Church and a day of feasting and celebration.

From here, take the public footpath opposite the entrance of the inn, which leads across fields, affording fine views to the south and southeast. Keep close to the hedge, and after crossing some stiles, the path will lead you to the church of St. Martin's. It was mainly built c.1200, although the nave contains some Anglo-Saxon stonework; the church was extensively altered in 1850 and 1864 with only the tower and other perp-endicular work left untouched. The 14th century tower has crenellations, and the large porch has the Roses of York and Lancaster on show, as it is a Henry VII addition. The holes in the tower buttresses are very unusual, and there are fine

St Martin's at Bremhill, with the remounted medieval cross in the foreground.

winged dragon gargoyles up the tower, which we have found to be on churches on ley lines. Here and there you will see older stone work projecting from the base of the walls, indicating an earlier build.

Inside there is a fine window of King Alfred, and of St. George subduing a dragon, and the Crucifixion window behind the altar shows Mary the

Floor monument and Norman font in St. Martin's Church, Bremhill.

Mother and Mary Magdalene. A rood loft can be seen between the aisle and the chancel which contains lattice work carving. The chancel itself holds lavish memorials to the Hungerford family. A monument to Rev John Tounson stands before the communion rails. He was expelled by the Puritans from the vicarage and his stall in Salisbury Cathedral, but was later reinstated in 1660. He built and endowed the eight almshouses at Calne for local poor women in 1682 (see Walks 1 and 5). In front of the altar is a floor memorial (see image above, left) of a knight, whose crest bears scallop shells (the symbol of St. James of Compostela and of pilgrims) and engrailed crosses (a popular Knights Templar motif, well represented at Roslyn Chapel). The Norman font is as old as the church and has a simple decoration. The arcades of c.1200 were re-modelled in 1850. There are original bits of stained glass in the north east window of the north aisle, and the mosaic sanctuary floor dates from 1907; look out also for the character poking out his tongue on one of the bench ends!

Returning outside, look for the faint remains of the scratch dial on the side of the porch. Walk to the nearby churchyard cross, which is Grade II listed. The base is of the cross is medieval, but is capped with a c.18th century square sundial with a ball finial (image p. 98). North of tower look out for the Bewley monument, which is Grade II listed. It is a chest tomb c.1830, with a frieze with rosettes and plaques, and an inscription to Mary Bewley, who died in 1826.

Above: the village cross at Bremhill.
Below: the well house and pump.

Leaving the churchyard via the south gate you will come to the village cross (image above right), whose worn medieval steps are now capped with a more modern shaft and cross head. This is a good place to sit and ponder all the people that will have done likewise over many hundreds of years.

The Village Hall nearby was formerly a school and

teacher's house, and dates from the mid-19th century, built by Thomas Poynder.

Now walk north down the hill, where a small roofed structure will be found on the right. This is a c.1875 well house that covers the old well (image

above), which still retains the old water pump, although sadly no longer working. The houses either side of the well are dated 1872, and others nearby are 1874. Opposite the well, examine all sides of the nearest building of Brook Farm, which has decorative heads reset into the walls (image left), as well as a bagpipe-playing bear, a goat, a rose, and a fish/dolphin.

Continue down the road and take the path in between houses 32 and 33 (the PFP sign is low down on a fence post). Follow this track between the houses, passing a well on the right, and soon a kissing gate is reached, which takes you into open fields. You can now see Calne in the distance. Follow the path across the fields, crossing stiles, a metal footbridge over Cowage Brook, then up a rise and back down the other side to a wooden bridge spanning Fisher's Brook. Both of these bridges can afford good sightings of dragonflies and damselflies during summer months. After the second bridge, go straight ahead through some trees and continue on to the main road, next to Lickhill Farm. Cross the road and then follow the signposted PFP, which wends itself between new houses, eventually coming to a roundabout. Follow Lickhill Rd south to return to the centre of Calne.

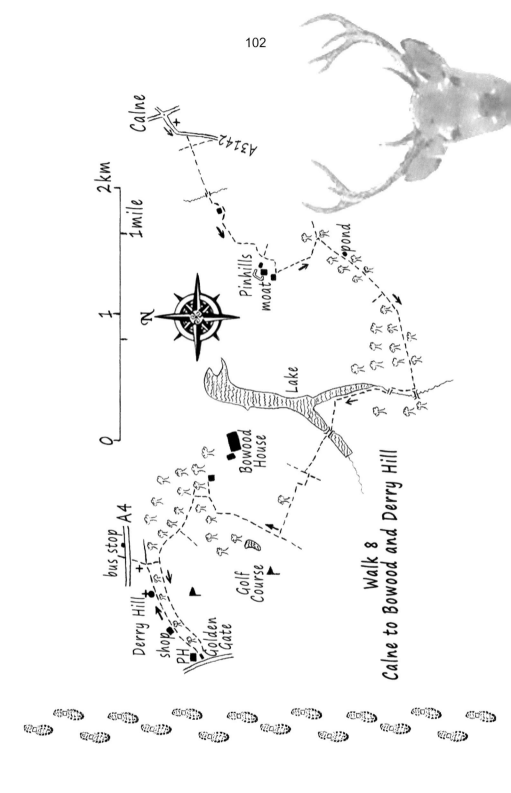

Walk 8
Calne to Bowood and Derry Hill

Calne

A3142

Pinhills
moat

pond

Lake

2km

1mile

N

1

0

Bowood
House

bus stop A4

Derry Hill

shop

PH

Golden
Gate

Golf
Course

Walk 8.
Calne to Bowood and Derry Hill

Summary of Walk 8

Distance: 7km (approx. 4¼ miles).
Circular or linear: linear.
Start point: The Green, Calne.
End point: bus stop on A4, Derry Hill (see buses below).
Degree of difficulty: easy walking; only mild slopes.
Restrictions: Pub opening, and Bowood House has seasonal openings.
Boots/wellies required: stout footwear only.
Public transport back to start point: Bus services 33, 33x and 55.
Wheelchair accessible: unsuitable for wheelchairs.
Refreshments and toilets: near the end is the Lansdowne Arms, village
   stores at Derry Hill, and a toilet for public use in Christ Church.
OS Explorer Map: 156.

This walk goes through the magnificent grounds of Bowood House, and on to Derry Hill. Wide open spaces, the lake and the chance to see buzzards overhead and roaming deer add to this walk, which, for the most part, is a tranquil experience.

From the southwest corner of The Green, cross the road to Silver Street. You will soon encounter the Methodist Church. Methodism came to Calne in 1808, and the first place they met was in a cottage in Curzon Street. They then moved to Kew Lane, at the end of Anchor Road, in what used to be a weaving shop. This building quickly became too small for their numbers and it was decided to build a chapel at 'the Quarry', although the exact location of this place is unknown. Then, in 1876, Lord Lansdowne provided a piece of land in Silver Street and a Wesleyan Chapel was built. There was also a

Primitive Methodist society formed in 1830 and they met in Back Row and later in London Road. In late 1965 both these congregations came together in the Silver Street building.

Continue along the pavement for a while, before turning right into Wenhill Lane, just before Guides hut. Follow this well defined track between houses, until the scenery eventually changes to open countryside. Along this track a small cottage is soon reached and the footpath diverts around the south side of it; around the far side it runs along the top of a low embankment. Cross the small bridge and stile and ascend to the hilltop dwellings known as Pinhills. The trees towards the right (north) side conceal an ancient moat. Pinhills was recorded in 1407 and the former Pinhills House stood on a rectangle enclosed by the moat. In December 1644 it was captured by Royalist forces, rendering it uninhabitable, and it was probably partly demolished. It was restored after the Civil War, for in 1728 a large house again stood on the moated site. It was at Pinhills that Dr Ingen Housz demonstrated to Dr Jenner that the use of a cowpox vaccination could be used to fight smallpox.

From here look back and you will see fine views of Calne, including St. Mary's tower, the Cherhill White Horse and the Lansdowne Monument. Just before Pinhills the path is diverted south, via stiles, and on reaching the tarmac drive turn left, following the footpath signs and the drive

Small footbridge with cascading waters at Bowood Lake.

south, noting views of the White Horse and Morgan's Hill (denoted by two masts on the summit). On reaching the intersection with another drive, turn right and head west. This pleasant wooded walk passes a pond, and eventually descends to a bridge at the foot of the slope. Do not cross this bridge (we will do so on Walk 9 to Lacock), but rather go through the kissing gate on the right, just before the bridge; from hereon we follow the public footpath signs across the Bowood Estate, currently the family seat of Charles Petty-Fitzmaurice, 9th Marquis of Lansdowne. Note the small weir under the bridge. Another smaller bridge is soon encountered and crossed. Either side of this bridge (image above) we noted numerous deer footprints in the mud, as well as badger runs. This bridge also has a water cascade on the north side. Follow the signs to the right, as you skirt Bowood's main lake. The park is 940 acres and was landscaped in 1760-6 by Lancelot

Bowood Lake and Bowood House (extreme left).

'Capability' Brown, and the house has a famous 'Orangery' designed in 1769 by Robert Adam. It also houses a mid-19th century chapel, as well as Dr Priestley's Laboratory, in which he discovered oxygen in 1774. Dotted around the 40 acre lake are grottos, a temple, and a lovely cascade. The rhododendron walk brings in many visitors annually between May and June. In 2007 divers from Calne found the lost hamlet of Mannings Hill (abandoned in 1766 when a stream was dammed to create the lake).

The signs then divert you away from the lake and up a slope, and after the crest you head down to a kissing gate; beyond this cross the bridge/dam that divides two lakes. Here we saw a flock of eight herons chilling out on the grass above the lake! Go through the gate and up the slope,

A rather romantic old depiction of Bowood House, which can be seen hanging in the Lansdowne Arms.

and at the top follow the signs left and then right along the gravel track. Following the signs, go through the gate, turning right and soon left and head across the field towards the small copse. The path skirts by the trees and goes through more kissing gates until a tarmac drive is reached. Turn right and follow the drive which skirts the edge of the golf course. Good views of the White Horse and Morgan's Hill to the east are afforded. The signs then direct you into woods and downhill. At foot of the slope, after crossing a small footbridge, turn left following a well defined and quiet track, which goes through the woods and then skirts the golf course.

On exiting the woods, the path then follows iron railings, and to the right is a gap in the trees, which can be taken as a short cut to the A4 bus stops; this misses out the recommended visit to the Golden Gate, the pub and Derry Hill church). We advocate carrying on along the path, passing two welcome benches, until the Golden Gate is reached. Note the mermaid on the south side, gold painted emblems on the gates, and the Lansdowne coat of arms including figures of Pegasus on the north side; this bears the Latin –

Left: the Golden Gate of Bowood. Right: the Lansdowne coat of arms, bearing two winged Pegasus horses, and a beehive.

'Vertute Non Verbis', which means, 'Deeds not words'. The signage on the grass on the north side includes a centaur wielding a bow and arrow. The gate is illuminated at night, often seen from several miles away.

Opposite is the Lansdowne Arms, which is well recommended for its friendly service, good food and open fires. A date of 1843 is shown above the pub's entrance, and the pub sign shows two Pegasus, a centaur and a beehive, as we saw opposite. Inside the pub are old images of Bowood.

After refreshing yourself, you can catch bus nos. 33 or 33X that serve the village, with services to Calne and Chippenham. However, we

Christ Church at Derry Hill

recommend walking east along the main street of Derry Hill. According to the Ancient Monuments Record for Wiltshire, worked gold and silver was unearthed at Red Hill, Derry Hill (at grid ref 958708), which suggested a Roman temple site. The Village Stores/Post Office offers refreshments and snacks (usually open 8.30am-5.30pm, but closed lunchtime, afternoons on Tuesday and Saturday, and all day Sunday.). Further on, the older part of the school still has a bell in situ.

Soon Christ Church will be reached. Note the two yew arches in the church yard, as well as the tomb of the 5th Marquis and his wife in the very NE corner. The church is usually open most days, and inside can be found a toilet, which we were told is open for use by ramblers. Founded in 1839, Christ Church was originally a 'Chapel of Ease', and was dedicated the following year, that of Queen Victoria's wedding. The spire was provided for by the 3rd Lord Lansdowne, and is mounted on a tower that is tall in it's own right. The original organ was formerly in St Mary's Calne, and was moved here when the latter received a new one in 1842. The present organ is an 1862 replacement. There are three decorative stained glass windows; the one behind the altar dates from 1865 and depicts the Ascension in stunning colours; on the north side is an 1881 window commemorating John Spencer, head gardener of Bowood, and shows Jacob

and the angels ascending a ladder (image above); on the south side is a window commemorating the nearby sawmill at Studley, which was established in 1900, and in the 1940-50s was one of the main employers locally. The business once operated off London Road, where Oldbury Prior is today, until its relocation to Studley.

Returning to the road, continue east and you will come to the old Reading Room and, around the corner, the War Memorial, on which is depicted St George slaying a dragon (image left). A little further on stands the Baptist church, which is dated 1814. On arriving at the main road, turn right and cross over road for buses to Calne, or turn left for the bus stop for Chippenham; services 33 and 55 serve this road.

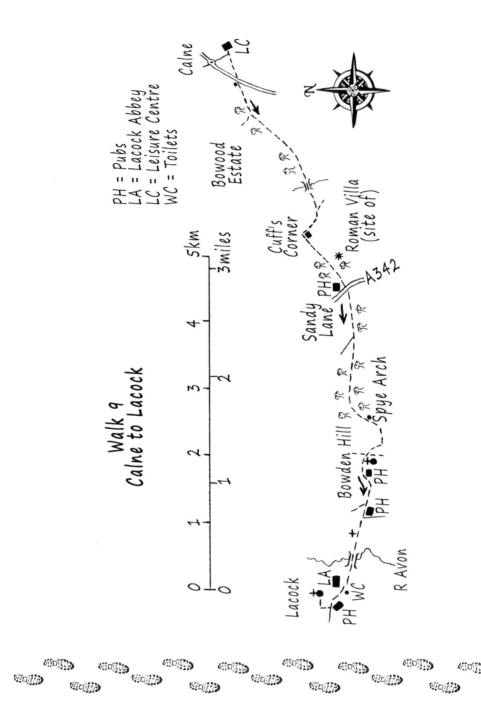

Walk 9
Calne to Lacock

PH = Pubs
LA = Lacock Abbey
LC = Leisure Centre
WC = Toilets

Walk 9.

Calne to Lacock

Summary of Walk 9

Distance: 10km (approx. 6 miles).
Circular or linear: linear.
Start point: The Leisure Centre, Calne.
End point: Lacock Church.
Degree of difficulty: easy walking; only mild slopes.
Restrictions: pub opening hours, and Lacock Abbey opening times.
Boots/wellies required: stout footwear recommended.
Public transport back to start point: bus 234 to Chippenham, then route 55 to Calne.
Wheelchair accessible: unsuitable for wheelchairs.
Refreshments and toilets: 4 pubs en route and toilets at Lacock.
OS Explorer Map: 156.

This walk goes west from Calne to Lacock. It passes through the quiet expanses of Bowood Estate via an 18th century coaching road, as well as passing four pubs en route (what's not to like!), and ending with the fascinating historic buildings and 'olde worlde' atmosphere of Lacock.

This walk begins outside Calne Leisure Centre, at the end of White Horse Way, Calne. There is a large car park, and there are toilets and a hot drinks vending machine in the centre.

From the entrance of the centre, head off to the far right corner of the car park and follow the track. This is a wide public footpath that passes the wildlife area created by pupils of John Bentley School. Cross the main road and take the drive opposite, passing Pillars Lodge; although marked 'Private Road', the drive is a public right of way on foot. This is the route of an old

Decorative bridge and weir at Bowood Lakes, over which this walk goes.

coaching road. After a while, ignore the turning to Pinhills, continuing straight on, noting the small pond on the left. After passing through woodland the track descends to an ornate bridge, built by 'Capability' Brown as part of his creation of Bowood's lakes. Water cascades over a weir on the north side. Cross the bridge and follow the public path that passes around the left (south) side of the cottage. We saw several deer footprints along this stretch. The path skirts the woods and then turns left behind Cuff's Corner Cottage, heading off SSW. There was a settlement at Cuff's Corner in 1709 and by 1728 a small farmstead and about 12 cottages existed. All except the farmstead had been removed by 1817, probably in the 1790s when the old coach road from Calne to Sandy Lane via Cuff's Corner went out of use when the route to Bath was altered.

This pleasant and quiet track then runs along the edge of woodland, the Great Wood, which has displays of snowdrops in January, Corallian grit underfoot, and a hollowed-out old yew. To the east there are glimpses of the Cherhill White Horse, Lansdowne Monument and Morgan's Hill.

As the path opens up on both sides (between two woods) look left (south) across the fields. In the far side of this field once stood Nuthills Villa, a Roman settlement on Nuthills Farm, discovered in 1924 when building debris obstructed ploughing. Excavations in 1924-6 uncovered a room with remains of painted wall-plaster, rough sandstone flooring and the probable base of a fountain. Fragments of flue and roofing tiles were also found.

Other finds included pottery, animal bones, a brooch, and coins. During field investigations in 1968, a scattering of Romano-British potsherds was noted on the surface of the ploughed field. Aerial photographs taken in 2013 revealed the crop mark traces of part of the plan of the villa buildings with an earlier curvilinear ditched enclosure, surrounded by the traces of a field system. This Roman settlement is not far north of nearby Verluccio, an important trading centre or posting station situated on the Roman road to Aqua Sulis (Bath); this is where Wans House stands today.

 Go through a gate as the A342 is approached, passing thatched cottages built to re-house the residents of Mannings Hill during the creation of the lakes. Horsepride Well Cottage still has a well in its grounds. On reaching the road, turn right to the George Inn (image below), the first of four pubs on

this walk. Built to serve the old Bath road, it was opened before 1720, and rebuilt in the 19th century. It offers a friendly service and is cosy, with both an open fire and a woodburner. It serves food, but enquiries should be made regarding restricted winter opening hours. Close by there was once a smithy, servicing the coaching horses. (Another local point of interest down the busy main road is Sandy Lane Church, which is unusual for a church in that it is thatched.)

Opposite the pub, take the road signposted for Lacock and Reybridge. We have now left Bowood land and approaching the Spye House Estate. In the valley to the south the Roman road runs parallel with the road along which you now walk. Stone pillars at White Lodge mark one entrance to Spye House, the latter of which is well hidden from view in the valley beyond. Bluebells carpet the adjacent woods in the spring. Please walk on the verges as much as possible along this stretch, because this old coach road is still a vehicular shortcut to Lacock today.

After the sharp bend, you will come to the grand entrances of both the Spye and Bowden Park Estates. On the left, the frontage of Spye Arch was actually taken from the gateway of Stanley Abbey (see walk 7). The family coat of arms has since been added, but look for the alcoves, which would once have housed religious statues, and also the dragons and other winged creatures below the arms. The arch stands on the Wessex Astrum (Knight and Perrott 2008). Opposite is the grand stone entrance to Bowden Park,

Spye Arch, Bowden Hill. This was originally the medieval gateway of Stanley Abbey, west of Calne. Above: detail of the coat of arms, and winged creatures beneath.
(Also see image on p. 8).

whose house is as equally well hidden from view.

Continue down the road, taking care to walk on the left side of the road around the sharp right bend. Around the corner the vista opens up, with magnificent views west across the valley of the River Avon. The Griffin Estate on the left is the home of Wiltshire Scrapstore, the arts and crafts

centre that recycles unwanted domestic and industrial items to sell, and use in creative workshops.

Bewley Common opens up in front of you and by the road is a milestone from the old coaching days, telling us that it is 14 miles to Bath (image left).

Beyond this is St. Anne's, a Victorian church founded 1857 by Captain John Gladstone RN, the older brother of Prime Minister William Gladstone. It is constructed of Bath stone, and has a nicely decorated porch, with foliated lions on each corner; look up and you will also see winged creatures adorning the tower. Inside are windows depicting St. George and St. Patrick (although the church is often locked). Around the back of the church, on the south side, is a convenient bench where one can take a quiet break, admiring distant panoramas.

Opposite the church is a well-house, fed by a stream whose source is a spring close by to the east. Continue down the road to the Rising Sun pub.

St. Anne's at Bowden Hill is positioned to offer imposing views over the Avon valley below.

We thought this name somewhat ironic as its views are mainly towards the setting sun! The conservatory and rear gardens afford great views over the land below. The road then descends steeply to the Avon floodplain. Near the bottom is a development called Bewley Edge, which are dwellings constructed of timber and glass by Huf Haus, environmentally sustainable kit houses from Germany.

The course of the old Wilts and Berks Canal once passed nearby and there was a brewery and a wharf here. Further along you will find the Bell Inn (restricted opening in winter), and the last building on the right before the river was formerly a chapel; now a private dwelling, it has a fine horse weathervane. The road then narrows as it crosses the two bridges that span the Avon (image left). Drainage holes in the walls take away flood waters that periodically consume the road, as happened during the wet winter of 2013-4. On the other side of the bridge the boardwalk and the pavement beyond offers good views of Lacock Abbey, a country house with monastic roots. It was originally founded as an Augustinian nunnery in

Above; the bridge over the River Avon at Lacock.
Below: Lacock Abbey from the south.

1232 by Ela, Countess of Salisbury. Following the Reformation it was developed into a grand house, and the famed octagonal tower dates from 1550. During the English Civil War the house was garrisoned by Royalists, who surrendered within days of Devizes being captured in 1645. Its medieval cloisters (with Green Man bosses) have been used for film sets, such as in the Harry Potter movies.

Another of Lacock's claims to fame is that it was the home of William Henry Fox Talbot. He invented the photographic negative process in 1835 and there is a museum here dedicated to him. Lacock Abbey is managed by the National Trust and is open all year as an optional addition to this walk; it has a museum, tea room and shop. The entrance is housed in what was once a large barn.

The Tithe Barn at Lacock.

In the car park opposite the NT entrance is a tea room and public toilets. Next door is the Red Lion, which has outdoor seating and accommodation.

Across the road from the pub's main entrance, turn right and go along East Street. The large wooden doors of the Tithe Barn will be found on the right and the building is open most days. Within are massive, old wooden beams (image above) and an information board. The barn is 14th century and was probably built into the precinct walls of Lacock Abbey.

Next to the barn is the village lock-up, a tiny structure with an orb on its roof. Beyond that are allotments, and next to these the village hall (which was formerly a school). At the end of the lane turn right at the Carpenters Arms. You will soon see King John's Hunting Lodge, now a tea room and a

B&B, and said to be the oldest building in Lacock; we can personally recommend the tea and cakes here!

The Lady Chapel at St. Cyriac's. This medieval chapel is very atmospheric. And has finely ornate stonework (below).

The final stop is the church of St. Cyriac. This is an unusual dedication in this country but one that is common in Normandy. Cyriac was a 3-year-old child who was martyred by the Governor of Cilicia in 303 AD. There was a Saxon church on this site but the present building dates from around 1480. As one enters there is a carving of a sun and moon overhead, and we found the 15th century Lady Chapel to be the most atmospheric part; it is the mortuary chapel of the Sharington and Talbot families of Lacock Abbey. The ceiling retains ornate carvings and original paintwork; under the arch is a face under a crescent moon, surrounded by hexagram stars (image left).

Nearby, behind the prayer candle stand, is a mythical head emerging from the bottom of the column, and a monument in the same chapel displays two opposing griffins. One window elsewhere shows Joseph of Arimathea, of Glastonbury fame, whilst yet another depicts three female figures portraying mercy, justice and humility; this is a fine example of the early Church adopting pre-existing Pagan symbolism, in this case the Triple Goddess.

St. Cyriac's (image below) is full of nice energies and displays ornate esoteric carvings. The church in fact stands on an alignment of sacred sites of the

Wessex Astrum, the huge landscape hexagram. This particular line runs from Brockley Cave, near Bristol, through sacred sites and churches at Whitchurch, Keynsham, Little Solsbury Hillfort, Box, Gastard, through Lacock, and on to the Cherhill White Horse and Avebury (Knight & Perrott, 2008).

Next to church is Lacock Pottery, well worth a visit to appreciate local artisan craftsmanship. The walk back to the bus stop is down Church Street, passing 'olde worlde' buildings (image below) — and one can get the feeling

of having stepped back in time. It has been used as film sets; one version of Pride and Prejudice was filmed here.

At the end of the street you will see the George Inn across the road. The bus stop is next to the pub and has a quaint bus shelter. From here, buses to Chippenham (service 234) are usually every hour. The connection to Calne (service 55) is made at Chippenham bus station.

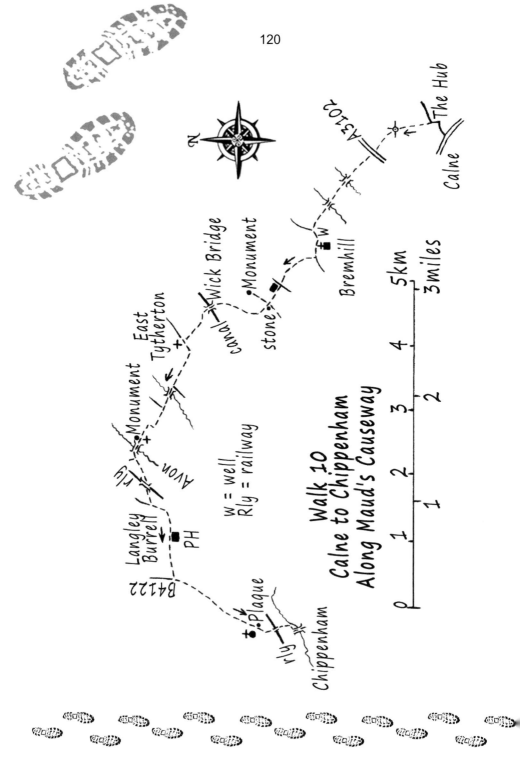

Walk 10
Calne to Chippenham
Along Maud's Causeway

The Hub

Calne

A3102

Bremhill

W

•Monument
stone

Wick Bridge

canal

East
Tytherton

Monument

+

Avon

rly

Langley
Burrell

PH

B4122

•Plaque

Chippenham

rly

W = well
Rly = railway

0   1   2   3   4   5km

1   2   3miles

Walk 10.
Calne to Chippenham
Along Maud's Causeway

Summary of Walk 10

Distance: 12km (approx. 7½ miles).
Circular or linear: linear.
Start point: The Community Hub, Calne.
End point: Chippenham.
Degree of difficulty: easy walking; mild slopes up to Bremhill, steep road down from Bremhill.
Restrictions: pub opening hours.
Boots/wellies required: stout footwear recommended.
Public transport back to start point: bus service 55 back to Calne.
Wheelchair accessible: unsuitable for wheelchairs.
Refreshments and toilets: pub at Langley Burrell & toilets at Chippenham.
OS Explorer Map: 156.

This walk follows much of the route of Maud Heath's Causeway between Bremhill and Chippenham. We were surprised by how much of the 15th century Causeway survives, and there are also commemorative monuments and stones en route to mark its creation and benefactor.

We begin outside the Community Hub, on the High St. From here walk north along North St, which eventually becomes Lickhill Rd. At the roundabout go straight ahead, but on the other side immediately take the path to the left, behind the 'Lickhill Rd' sign. Follow the path as it bears right and head along Kennet Walk, between the new houses, a hedge and old walls. At the main road (A3102 Calne Ring Road), go straight across, and navigate the stiles of the signposted public footpath. This path goes west to Bremhill village, which can soon be seen on the skyline ahead. After crossing the first stream (Fisher's Brook) ascend the path briefly before passing through the hedge via a stile on the left. Turn right and descend the slope to the metal bridge that crosses Cowage Brook. Follow the path up to Bremhill, which stands on the crest of the hill.

As you pass the first cottages note the well on the left. On reaching the road, turn left, whereby the village well, complete with redundant pump, will soon be encountered (see image p. 100). The building opposite has various stone heads and creatures mounted into the walls (see image p. 101). Continue to the medieval cross and the church (see Walk 7).

Continue along the road around the right side of the churchyard, following the pavement. Ignore the 'Lodowicks' turn off and continue uphill until the signposted PFP is taken on the right. Once through the gate, follow the path down to the stream, heading initially in the direction of the telegraph pole in the field (keeping all the 'Private – No Right of Way' signs to your left).

Cross the stream and ascend the slope to the gate. Continue along a now well-defined path, pausing to look behind to admire the fine views of the Cherhill White Horse, the Lansdowne Monument, Morgan's Hill, and of Calne in the valley below. Cross the stile next to Mount Farm, and continue straight ahead until the road is reached. Cross over

Plaque on standing stone at the top of Wick Hill.

and go straight ahead down the lane opposite, marked 'East Tytherton and Chippenham'. After passing Monument Farm, you will arrive at the top of the steep descent that is Wick Hill. On the left is a tall stone set into the hedge, commemorating Maud Heath (images above and below).

Maud Heath's Causeway is a track from Bremhill to Chippenham, part of

which rises above the Avon floodplain on 64 brick arches. The causeway was the gift of the eponymous Maud Heath, who made her fortune carrying eggs to market at Chippenham. Maud was a lady of considerable means who lived in the valley below during the latter part of the 15th century. She was a childless widow, and when she died, "... in the year of grace 1474, for the good of travellers did bestow in land and houses the sum of eight pounds a year foreer to be laid out on a causeway leading from Wick Hill to Chippenham Clift", some of which was the very route along which she had tramped to market every week for most of her life. It was her wish that income from her land be used to construct the causeway to enable villagers to cross the Avon floodplain and reach the Chippenham markets with, "... all their goods to sell, and dry feet". Over 500 years later a charity still maintains the path out of her bequest.

In early accounts the Causeway is called a 'causey'. This may be a corruption of the French 'chausée', meaning a road with a laid surface. There is evidence that the original Causeway was surfaced with a mixture of limestone brash and cobbling for much of its length, providing a dry walking surface rather than a raised walkway. Fragments of cobbling can still be seen at various places along this walk, protruding between modern tarmac.

This marker stone has stood here since 1827, identifying the start of the Causeway. Originally the inscription was in Latin, but was subsequently replaced by a translation into English (images p. 122-3), credited to the vicar of Bremhill, Rev. William Bowles. The inscription reads: *'From this Wick Hill begins the praise Of Maud Heath's gift to these highways'.*

Opposite the stone, go through gate and cross the field (a bridleway) to Maud Heath's Monument. Atop of the tall column sits the statue of a lady, Maud Heath herself no less. The monument was erected in 1838, positioned so that Maud can look over the floodplain across which is traced her Causeway; she wears a bonnet and authentic market day clothes. It was erected by the great Whig Henry, Lord Lansdowne, and features a poem by the critic William Lisle Bowles, who was vicar of Bremhill. The inscription near the base reads:

Maud Heath's Monument at Bremhill, erected in 1838. Maud's statue overlooks the Avon floodplain, over which traverses her causeway.

"Thou who dost pause on this aerial height
Where Maud Heath's Pathway winds in shade and light
Christian wayfarer in a world of strife
Be still and consider the Path of Life".

There is a bench here, affording both an opportunity to rest and very fine views across the Avon and Marden valley to Chippenham and the Cotswolds beyond; we have seen badgers here at dusk. In the opposite direction the Cherhill White Horse is again visible.

Return to road and turn right, descending the hill. A small standing stone is soon passed. The pavement you are walking along is the start of Maud's Causeway, which even today is the basis of an almost continuous pavement from here to Chippenham. The bench halfway down the hill offers fine views; the distant church spire is that of St. Paul's in Chippenham. Keep your eyes peeled, for at various places in the next 3¾ miles (6km) one glimpses the original stone cobbles underfoot, as well as old kerbstones, such as when walking through Bremhill Wick, where they are periodically visible. At Wick Bridge, just beyond house no. 57, the old Wilts and Berks Canal can be seen, which still holds water.

Further along the road the green at East Tytherton will be reached. A bench

behind the modern sundial is a good resting place. Opposite is the Moravian Church (image left), sandwiched between two houses. It has a small bell tower and is dated 1792 (although a church was established here in 1743). The Moravians were originally called the Bohemian Brethren and have their roots in the 15th century; the Moravian Episcopal Church was recognised by an Act of Parliament in 1749. A sign here states that it was, '… originally a preaching place of the 18th century evangelist John Cennick'. He was one of John Wesley's first lay preachers until a split in 1745, when he became a Moravian. Through his work in the village, Cennick became one of the founders of the Moravian Church in England. It was here that he built the Clergyman's House, the Chapel and a boarding school for girls.

From here follow the road marked 'Langley Burrell', passing the Maud Heath Centre, used now by the Girl Guides. Following the pavement means you are back on Maud's Causeway. Around the bend the pavement moves to the other side of the road, passing Causeway House. After this it changes sides again, and a long straight stretch of road follows; a welcome bench can be found near the turning to Stanley. More original stones can be seen underfoot at the entrance to Barnbridge B&B. The bridge beyond crosses the Cade Burna, a tributary of the Avon.

The sign denoting you are entering Kellaways is also the boundary of the Calne Community Area. St. Giles Church at Kellaways is a surprising gem, a small chapel complete with bell tower and weather vane (image below and Colour Plate 11). The church is fairly isolated and close to the road and Maud Heath's Causeway. The interior can be viewed through windows on the south side, where the font, small pipe organ and wooden altar may be glimpsed. The first recorded rector was Edmund of Tytherton in 1304, when the church was under the patronage of the Calloway family, who remained patrons until 1429. Legend has it that there was a plague of rats in the old church, which caused its abandonment and the construction of a new one; rats cavorted throughout services, reminding us of the Pied Piper of Hamelin! Whatever the truth of the matter the old church had probably become dilapidated and it was decided it would be easier to build a new one, on or near the same site, than repair the old.

The present church was built c.1800 with box pews, which were later replaced in the late 19th century with wooden pews, when the west gallery

Above: St. Giles at Kellaways, next to Maud's Causeway. Below: Monument with sundial at Kellaways Bridge.

was also removed. The pulpit and ashlar font are both 18th century and presumably came from the earlier church.

Soon after the church, Maud Heath's wonderful elevated causeway, with arches beneath, can be crossed. You will be elevated some 5ft above the road as the River Avon is traversed. This was rebuilt in 1811 over a series of 64 arches. Part of this was again replaced with a road bridge in 1853, which was in turn rebuilt in 1961.

At the start of the bridge, a monument dated 1698 celebrates Maud's legacy; three sundials tell us the time, and directions to 'Chippenham Clift' and 'Wick Hill' are indicated. Other script reminds us of the date of construction – 1474. The sundial is inscribed 'Tempus Volat' ('time flies') on the eastern side and 'Dum tempus habemus operemur bonum' ('While we have time let us do good') on the south; on the west side is the inscription, 'Redibo – tu numquam' ('I shall return – you shall not'). The river can be accessed via stone steps at the east end of the bridge, opposite the monument.

The raised section of Maud's Causeway, rebuilt in the 19th century (see also Colour Plate 12).

Beyond the river, continue along the causeway pavement, through the tunnel under the railway and beyond. Just before the sign telling that you have reached Langley Burrell, a bench is provided, next to a small stream that passes under the road. Passing through the village, more old stones are exposed underfoot, and look out for a field with alpacas! Langley Green House, set back on the left, is built of Bath Stone, a Grade II listed Georgian residence built over the remains of Maud Heath's house, which dated from the 12th century, and where she died in 1474.

The Langley Tap pub is a welcome stop, with a good atmosphere, an open fire, wood burner and fine food. Next door is a house called the Old Brewery, a relic of the site of Slades Brewing House, which is marked on an 1899 map that hangs in the pub. The pub's nickname of 'The Tap' comes from the fact that for many years the pub stood adjacent to the brewery, so the beer was said to always be 'on tap'.

At the B4069, turn left in the direction of Chippenham and continue along the pavement. As we entered the town along Langley Road we were surprised to see more surviving cobble stones and kerbstones underfoot. At the entrance to the Parsonage Way Industrial Estate old kerbstones reveal themselves to a keen eye. Continuing downhill along Langley Road we found the final old kerbstones outside no. 73, just before a new development called Maud Heath Court — a fitting tribute. Just before the busy roundabout, St.

Paul's church stands on the right, the spire of which we saw earlier from Wick Hill. It was designed by George Gilbert Scott and was built in 1854-55. In front of the last building before the roundabout, next to road signage, is a memorial plaque to Maud Heath (image left), mounted on a white-painted stone, marking the end of the Causeway.

Turn left and go along Old Road. Cross the railway bridge, and on the other side turn right and walk between the two car parks. Cross the road and take Monkton Hill opposite. This descending road comes out at the stone pillars of Monkton Park. Go through this grand entrance and immediately take the steps on the right down to the River Avon. Turn right at the bottom and follow the path to the bridge. At the main road, the bus back to Calne (no. 55) can be caught around the corner to the right. Otherwise you can cross the bridge and experience Chippenham's many cafes and shops, eventually catching the bus at the bus station.

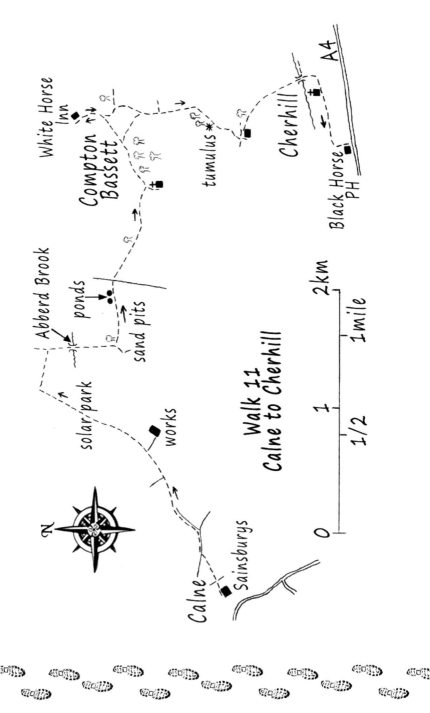

Walk 11
Calne to Cherhill

Walk 11.

Calne to Cherhill

Summary of Walk 11

Distance: 8.2km (approx. 5 miles).
Circular or linear: linear.
Start point: entrance to Sainsbury's, Calne.
End point: Black Horse pub, Cherhill.
Degree of difficulty: mainly easy walking; some steeper slopes between Compton Bassett and Cherhill.
Restrictions: opening hours of two pubs and café.
Boots/wellies required: stout footwear recommended.
Public transport back to start point: bus service L4 to Calne.
Wheelchair accessible: unsuitable for wheelchairs.
Refreshments and toilets: pubs at Compton Bassett and Cherhill, and the Divine Café near the end.
OS Explorer Map: 157.

This walk is through quiet, rural countryside, and links Calne, Compton Bassett and Cherhill.

Starting outside Sainsbury's in Calne town centre, proceed down the alleyway that skirts the northern car park, taking you down the side of supermarket. Cross the road at the end of alley and go down Broken Cross. Turn right at Abberd Way and soon take a left to follow Abberd Way as it changes direction. The tarmac soon runs out at a gate, and a bridleway mark is on back of a sign stating, 'Private Road No Entry'. Walk along this track, through the next gate, and continue straight on when a road joins from the left. Ignore the entrance to Hills Quarry and continue along the track ahead, passing the new Solar Park. At the top of the slope turn right into the field, and follow the public footpath alongside the hedge, which skirts along the north end of the new Solar Park. Calne can be proud that its 'Green' credentials have been enhanced by this large installation, which was designed to be virtually imperceptible from the neighbouring countryside and local housing.

At the far end of the field, go through an opening and turn right, joining a bridleway that heads south. Cross the concrete bridge that spans the Abberd Brook, continuing directly ahead and uphill. At the top, the path bends right and does a dog-leg around a small copse called Andrews' Patch. Immediately after the copse, turn left to join a well-defined track. Go left (east) and follow the track (marked cycle route) around the perimeter of the quarry and landfill site (this route varies from that shown on older OS maps). Passing two large ponds, the road will soon be reached. Cross the road and go straight ahead to Compton Bassett. We noted deer in the fields along this stretch.

At a sharp bend, just beyond two delightful thatched cottages (image right and Colour Plate 8),

take the track to the right next to a small post box; this leads up to the church, which stands on a small knoll, and to Compton Bassett House. The original house was built c. 1670 by Sir John Weld, but was demolished in 1931-3. The present house was once owned by the famous architect Sir Norman Foster (now Baron Foster of Thames Bank) of "The Gherkin" fame, who sold it in 1992. In 2008 the singer-songwriter Robbie Williams purchased the property for £7 million, which included gamekeeper lodgings,

a tennis court, helipad and extensive grounds. To the SW of the church are the old stables dating from 1665, built to a very high quality.

Inside St. Swithin's Church is a notable, ornately carved rood screen, and a finely carved stone pulpit (image right). Stained glass windows include scenes of the Last Supper, and St. John the Divine with a serpent in a chalice. Other windows, dated 1885, show St. Catherine with long golden hair and her Catherine Wheel, and St. George slaying the dragon. Behind the altar is depicted the Crucifixion, which has Mary Magdalene ('companion' of Jesus) in close attendance, and there is also a pleasant Lady Chapel.

Above: fine stonework inside St. Swithin's. Below: Windows showing St. George and St. Catherine.

Returning to the lane, turn right and follow the road through the village. Views soon open up westwards over the small vale of the Abberd Brook. Continuing along the road will take you by some cottages dated 1868, and the old school house, which retains its bell.

Follow the pavement to the White Horse Inn (image below), which has a painting of the horse above the entrance, as well as a small image of the

Uffington White Horse. This award-winning, 18th century inn is a convenient stop and offers a friendly service. In times gone by, tug of war competitions were held outside.

Retrace your steps back along the road, southwards, and soon take a track going off to the left, marked bridleway. Just beyond the cottages leave the main track and take the PFP on the right, which goes through a small gully. Up this path we saw several badger setts, as well a more deer in the adjacent fields. Further on, ignore the two gates either side and continue uphill via the pretty, and probably ancient, sunken track; fragments of chalk can be seen among tree roots. A

Bronze Age tumulus in Mount Wood.

well-defined track soon diverges from the right; continue uphill along this track, walking over the outcropping chalk rock.

On reaching more open ground, continue ahead (south) to the top of the hill, passing through a gate. Follow the path around the edge of the field that skirts Mount Wood. There are fine southerly views to the Cherhill White Horse, Oldbury Hillfort and the Lansdowne Monument, this time viewed from around a similar height, which is unusual. About half way along note the well preserved mound to your right at the edge the woods (image above). This is a 10ft high Bronze Age burial mound, shown as a 'tumulus' on the OS map.

The track then gradually descends and on reaching the road turn left (east), passing farm buildings. Continue along this lane, which descends to the village of Cherhill, with fine views of the White Horse and the Lansdowne Monument (image left), with Cherhill village in the valley below. At the foot of the hill cross the bridge that spans a very youthful River's Brook, which goes on to feed the Marden at Quemerford. Then turn right at the road junction, following the

signposted cycle route to the Church.

Cherhill is a lovely, sleepy village, nestled in the River's Brook valley. The Manor House, located next to the church, dates from 1699, and fragments of Roman mosaic were found in the grounds (see image p. 6). Although sadly gone, a large tithe barn once

stood adjacent the church; it was 110ft long with two porches, and a date of 1425 was found on one of the timbers. It was demolished in 1956 due to its poor state of repair.

The church (image previous page) is dedicated to St. James of Compostela, the patron saint of pilgrims, which seems fitting as we approach the end of this walk. Inside, a finely carved wooden reredos behind the altar depicts the Annunciation and the Holy Birth. The east altar window shows Christ in Majesty, surrounded by a heavenly host of harp-playing angels. Walls either side of the altar show exposed bricks of white chalk. Look for the colourful banner (image above) of St. James, wearing a scallop shell, his emblem. The banner also depicts wheat, a sheep, the church, the White Horse and the Monument. Returning outside, turn right and note how the church tower leans markedly to one side; you can also view the old buildings of the Manor House. Under your feet is also the site of a Roman villa.

Back at the road turn right, and follow the lane that passes quaint thatched cottages and the old school, with the bell still hanging in the bell tower. Next door is the Village Hall, with a fine array of solar panels on the roof, the results of a commendable community project. Continue along the road until you reach a development of dwellings called 'The Orchard', where you should turn left. At the far end of this short lane, cross over and take the public footpath between the post box and the notice board. This leads to the

Black Horse Pub, a friendly establishment which serves fine food (check their website for opening hours).

On the A4, almost opposite the pub, stands the thatched Millennium bus shelter (image below and p. 145), complete with a local sarsen stone sundial beneath. From this stop you can get a bus back to Calne (Route L4 – which has a very restricted service at times – check timetables, for you may have to book in advance!). Alternatively, you can walk west along the A4 a few hundred metres to the excellent Divine Café, which is where the next walk begins.

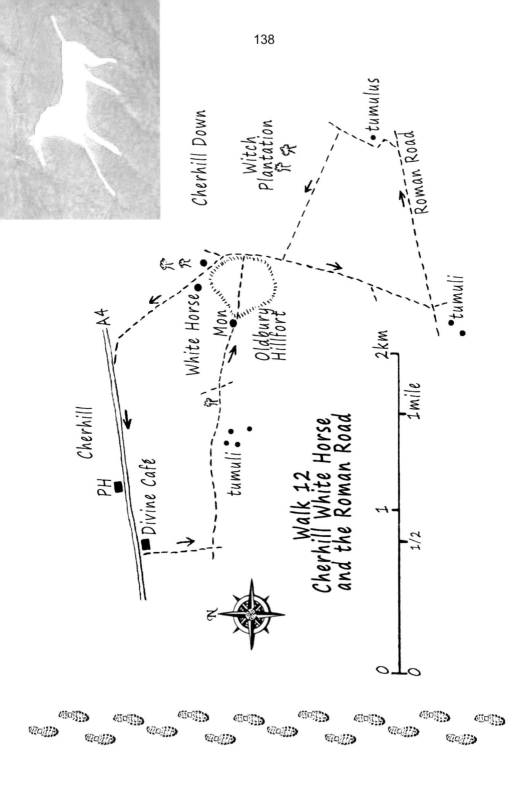

Cherhill Down

Witch Plantation

tumulus

Roman Road

A4

White Horse

Mon

Oldbury Hillfort

tumuli

Cherhill

PH

Divine Café

tumuli

Walk 12
Cherhill White Horse and the Roman Road

N

0 — 1/2 — 1 — 2km
0 — 1/2 — 1mile

Walk 12.

Cherhill White Horse & the Roman Road

Summary of Walk 12

Distance: 8.5km (5¼ miles).
Circular or linear: circular.
Start point and end point: Divine Café .
Degree of difficulty: some steep inclines up to the Monument, and a
   moderate incline back up Cherhill Hill later on.
Restrictions: opening hours of the pub and café.
Boots/wellies required: stout footwear recommended.
Public transport: bus service L4 back to Calne (no Sunday service).
Recommendation: preferable on weekend, when A4 is quieter.
Refreshments and toilets: The Black Horse, and the Divine Café at
   both the start and the end.
OS Explorer Map: 157.

This walk takes in stunning scenery, with spectacular views from the top of
the chalk downland. It also includes two of North Wiltshire's well known
landmarks, as well as a walk along the Roman road.

Start at the Divine Café, an excellent stop for cream teas and lunches.
Immediately next to the café, on the west side, take the bridleway south
from the A4. This path gently ascends, and at the intersection of another
bridleway, turn left (east). This path is old and sunken in places, and in fact
follows the course of an alignment that runs from Brockley Cave (near
Bristol) to Avebury, one of the lines of the Wessex Astrum (Knight and
Perrott, 2008). It is the same alignment on which stands St. Peter's at
Blackland. Further on, when another track crosses the path, turn right and
then almost immediately take a left over the stile. A sign shows that you

are entering National Trust/SSSI land. The scenery soon opens up and soaring buzzards are commonly seen riding the thermals. Look out for the various species of blue butterflies, as well as delicate chalkland flowers. Follow the track towards the tree clump and the Lansdowne (or Cherhill) Monument beyond. You may get glimpses to the south of Bronze Age burial mounds, showing how the hill was sacred back in prehistory, confirmed by Neolithic finds here. Walking around the right side of the trees, there is a good view of the Monument with the White Horse to its left (image below and Colour Plate 10).

The Cherhill White Horse was cut in 1780, and is the second oldest of Wiltshire's chalk horses, and the third oldest in England. It was scoured under the direction of Dr Christopher Alsop, of Calne, who designed it to be elongated to resemble the horses of the artist George Stubbs, a friend of Alsop. Its construction has to be admired, as the slope is steep, around 45°, plunging dramatically from the Iron Age ramparts above. It measures 157ft long and 142ft high, and Dr Alsop apparently directed its creation with the use of a megaphone from a vantage point below. During WWII the horse was obscured so as not to be a navigation aid to German bombers, a fate that

The Cherhill White Horse from the west. The ramparts of
Oldbury Castle hillfort rise to the right.

also befell the Cerne Giant in Dorset (see Knight 2013). At one time, in the 19th century, glass bottles comprised the eye, making it glisten, whereas now the eye is made of dark concrete that stands proud of the surface. The horse was floodlit in 1937 for the Coronation. The hill figure was restored in 2002 and 2006, using 160 tons of compacted chalk, along with shuttering to hold the chalk in place. It also stands on the aforementioned alignment that continues to Avebury. It is surprising from how far away the horse is visible, as is obvious from some of the other walks.

Continue towards the monument via two gates. As you approach the obelisk you walk pass the embankments of the hillfort. The Lansdowne (or Cherhill) Monument was built in 1845 by the 3rd Marquis of Lansdowne, of Bowood House. The Grade II listed monument (image right) is a memorial to his ancestor, physician and surveyor Sir William Petty (1627–1684), and was designed by Charles Barry. It is 38m (125ft) high, built of Bath Stone, and is an easily recognised landmark, visible from miles away on some of our other walks. The fence and safety netting has been erected in recent years by the National Trust due to the poor state of repair of the monument. Although some repairs were undertaken in 1990, a sign here states that, '… it is not clear when funding will be available for this work.' We will comment no further on this sorry state of affairs, as this listed obelisk continues to crumble.

The views from the Monument are stunning, up to 25 miles on a clear day. To the SW, Morgan's Hill rises - its beech copse and two masts are well known landmarks; to the west Calne can be seen nestled in the valley of the River Marden, with the new solar park to the right; to the north Cherhill is below, next to the A4; close by to the east the ramparts of the hillfort rise; to the NE is Yatesbury church and old RAF aerodrome buildings; to the SE Tan Hill and Milk Hill, the two highest points in Wiltshire, are on the skyline.

From here take the well-defined path into the heart of the Oldbury Camp (or Castle) Iron Age hillfort, which stands at the lofty 260m

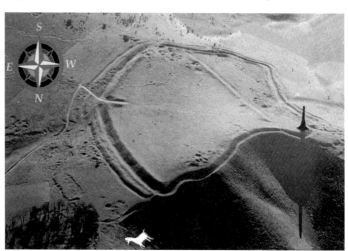

Aerial view of Oldbury Hillfort, the Monument and the White Horse. (From info boards on A4.)

(850ft) summit of Cherhill Hill. This roughly ovate enclosure, comprising 25 acres, was defended by two ditches with an entrance at the east end. Pottery from 2-3rd centuries BC was found here, and it has been advocated that a Roman temple may have stood here, suggested by finds of pottery and roof tiles found adjacent to the enclosure. The hillfort may have been a Saxon centre in the 5th – 6th centuries AD, as a Saxon brooch was found here; it is well attested that hillforts were sometimes re-occupied by the Saxon elite around this time.

Carry on ahead through the hillfort, and exit through the eastern entrance;

The view during the descent from Cherhill Hill. The dark line crossing left to right is the course of the Roman road. Four Bronze Age tumuli are in the field beyond, and the beech copse of Furze Knoll on Morgan's Hill stands on the skyline.

either side are deep ditches of the hillfort perimeter. Go straight ahead until a short post is reached, at which point go right (south), along a path that follows the Wessex Ridgeway. Go through the gate and proceed downhill, along a slightly sunken track. This affords great views south across the chalk downland, with Furze Knoll and Salisbury Plain on the skyline. Further down the slope, note the course of the Roman road marching across the land (image above), with a group of barrows just beyond. Go through the next gate, which defines the southern limit of the National Trust property. Continue down to the Roman track.

At the Roman road is an intersection of bridleways; turn left (east) and follow the ancient Roman way, a vital artery of the Empire linking Aqua Sulis (Bath) and Londinium (London). In places the track is still raised above the fields on

The Roman road marches across the landscape on its way to Bath. Morgan's Hill is on the skyline.

the south side and the ancient route marks the boundary between two parishes; it is a common practice for parish boundaries to be marked by ancient sites or tracks, as these were enduring places known since time immemorial. Further along the track note the mounds at the far side of the large field, alongside the A361 Devizes Road. These are called the *Three Barrows*, more Bronze Age burial sites. These barrows stand on the axis of the famous St Michael Line, the alignment of sacred sites that runs from Cornwall to East Anglia, via Glastonbury and the Neolithic henge of Avebury (Colour Plate 14).

At the next bridleway sign turn left and ascend the hill, passing a chalk pit. At the top of the slope there are great views to the east, to Silbury Hill, Knoll Down and the Marlborough Downs beyond (image below). Cross the stile on the left and then bear left up the hill, keeping close to the field boundary all the way. Further up the hill the Lansdowne Monument comes

into view ahead. In the valley to the north, Witch Plantation can be seen, and beyond that the tower of Yatesbury Church and the ruinous RAF aerodrome buildings. At the far end of the field, cross the stile and turn right (north), along the well-defined path (along which we walked earlier). At the small post, turn left and then right (before the hillfort banks), following the path north and heading to the left of the wood. On reaching the edge of the steep drop, you can glimpse the White Horse just a few feet below. From here, Calne and the church at Cherhill can be seen, and a water pumping station below. The path should then be followed downhill until it reaches the gravel track. From the cattle grid is a fine view back up to the White Horse. Follow the vehicular track to the main road, where there is an information board of facts about the White Horse (Colour Plate 10), the Monument, the hillfort, and Roman coins that have been

found locally. Cross over the road and follow the pavement downhill into Cherhill. The first building encountered was at one time the Bell Inn. It is dated as 'c.1726' near the front door; it was once a coaching stop and remained so until 1872.

You will also pass by the Old Rectory, the former police station, and the Black Horse

The stone sundial within the Millennium Shelter on the main road at Cherhill.

Pub, an 18th century coaching inn offering an a la carte menu and open fires; look for the painting depicting the infamous Cherhill Gang, a group of 18th century highwaymen who accosted their victims whilst completely naked! Cross over and explore the thatched shelter with its sarsen stone sundial (image above & p. 137). If time allows, visit Cherhill Church nearby (details on p. 135-6). Finally you will arrive back at the Divine Café, which affords a friendly welcome, and good food. The Café is usually open Wednesday to Sunday, 9.00am – 4.00pm.

On the same side of the road, 200m beyond the café, is a reminder of the London to Bath Road coaching days. A lonely, cracked milestone informs us it is, '85 miles from London, 21 to Bath' (image right). The road was turnpiked between 1743 and 1870.

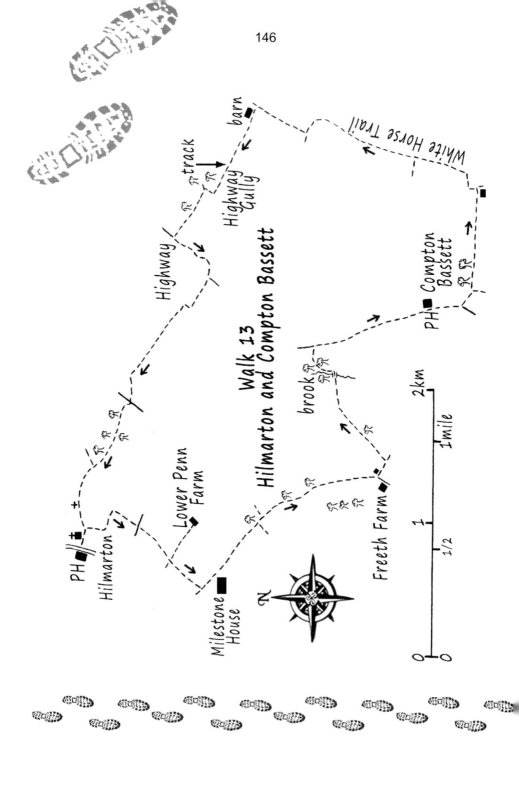

Walk 13
Hilmarton and Compton Bassett

barn

track

Highway

Highway Gully

White Horse Trail

Compton Bassett
PH

Milestone House

PH
Hilmarton

Lower Penn Farm

brook

Freeth Farm

N

0	1/2	1	1mile
0	1	2km	

Walk 13.
Hilmarton, Compton Bassett & Highway

Summary of Walk 13

Distance: 12.5km (7¾ miles).
Circular or linear: circular.
Start point and end point: The Duke, Hilmarton.
Degree of difficulty: mainly level walking, but a steep incline up to the downs from Compton Bassett.
Restrictions: opening hours of two pubs.
Boots/wellies required: stout footwear recommended.
Public transport: bus 55 Calne-Swindon service.
Wheelchair accessible: unsuitable for wheelchairs.
Refreshments and toilets: pubs at Hilmarton and Compton Bassett.
OS Explorer Map: 157.

This walk takes us along level land between Hilmarton and Compton Bassett, before climbing to the heights and elevated beauty and isolation of the chalk downland.

Local round barrows suggest an early occupation, and Roman occupation of Hilmarton parish is evident as numerous artefacts have been discovered from this period, including pottery, as well as roof tiles discovered on the site of the recently built school hall. The largest discovery from the Roman period was of a Romano-British well at nearby Corton. Two mills are mentioned in Hilmarton in the Domesday Book. One flour mill was believed to have been on the same site for at least 800 years before it was pulled down in 1915. There was also a windmill, last recorded in 1348. The earliest documented record of Hilmarton was in 962AD, and by 1086, during the Domesday survey, the three estates of Hilmarton, amounting to

11 hides, were held by Ralph under William of Eu. In 1611, Robert Baynard was granted livery of the manor with a fair. This was known as the Lammas Fair and was held annually for several hundred years. The estate was sold to the Poynder family in 1813. The family were the benefactors of much development in the village, including the almshouses, which we shall see later. Most of the original medieval buildings in Hilmarton were either destroyed by fire, demolished or completely remodelled during the 19th and 20th centuries. This was mainly due to the upgrade and modernisation of Poynder estate properties, until Lord Poynder sold off most of the estate in 1914.

The Duke, Hilmarton. The buildings to the right are an old brewery and coach house.

The Duke, on the main road, is our starting point. (Please only park in the car park if using the pub at the start or the end; there is on street parking near the church.) The Duke Inn was built between 1850-1860 and replaced the Duke of Wellington Inn which had been 'inappropriately located' next to the old church tower. The old stables and Arkell's brewery buildings are still to be seen today. It is rumoured that tunnels once ran

from the inn to the well at Fairmead. In the 18th century there were at least two drinking establishments in the village, The Duke of Wellington and the Broad Axe, the latter of which is believed to have been located next to the school.

Take time to explore the pub and its outbuildings. You can see the Duke of Wellington himself on the pub sign, and as a profile relief above the main entrance (image above). The date of 1843 is on front of the building, and next to the front door look for a small plaque that says, 'Air Raid Wardens' Post' (image below). At the entrance to the car park stands a very early petrol pump, painted black. The older buildings at the rear are the old brewery house, a coach house (arched entrances) and stables to the right in the corner of the car park. The brewery has a high hatch and louvre slatted windows for

ventilation, and the stables used to be the starting point of the local hunt. Near the side door is a mounted tap and basin; this was brought with the new landlords as it was a commemoration of a departed pet dog. Inside, you will find a stone fireplace, as well as a friendly service (check off-season opening times).

Above: St. Laurence Church. Below: The war commemoration window depicts St. George subduing a dragon, and Gordon of Khartoum.

Cross the road to the church of St. Laurence (image left and Colour Plate 4). The church is usually only open on Wednesday in the season, but the keys can be obtained at other times from No, 34 Church St (01249 760312) or from the Church Warden (01249 760401). The church is recorded from 1291, although the arches separating the Lady Chapel may date from c. 1200. The chancel walls are thought to date from the 14th century. A comprehensive renovation was undertaken in 1879 by William Poynder. Externally, note the clock, the finely ornate gargoyles on the tower and, here and there, older sections of stonework at the foot of the church.

Inside, there is much of interest. Fine stained glass windows variously depict Faith, Hope and Charity, St. George and the dragon, General Gordon of Khartoum, and Mary of Bethany (whom many researchers equate with Mary Magdalene). Pride of place probably belongs to an original King James Bible, dating

from 1611, which is housed in a glass case, with a mirror beneath to allow one to examine the oak cover. Close by is a grand 17th century memorial on the wall. Three more from this century can be found mounted on the wall near the font. Of interest is the top beam of the ornate painted rood screen, which was brought here from the church at Highway when it closed. The organ beyond is dated 1946. The painted wall behind the altar is unusual, as are the three wooden mounted coats of arms between the arches. Next to the pulpit is a colourful painting of the Crucifixion, with Mary Magdalene, curiously with her back to us, comforting Mary the Mother in her grief (image above).

Going back to the road through the lych gate, turn left and walk to the Primary School. This has a very ornate and slender bell tower (image next page), on which a plaque tells of how the bell was restored for the Queen's Silver Jubilee. Another plaque, less obvious under the front window, commemorates the planting of a rose bush 1937.

Turn right and follow Compton Rd. The corner buildings were the village shop and the post office. Post Office Cottage bears the date of 1876 and the Poynder coat of arms. Various cottages in the village bear dates between 1832-1876, and the initials of William H Poynder, the Lord of the Manor, can be seen on several houses. During Poynder's remodelling, friend and architect Henry Weaver designed and oversaw the building of a number of properties in the parish, most of which are now Grade II Listed. The Old Forge will soon be passed on your left, which was adjoined to an estate cottage in 1860. This building still retains some original 17th century features.

Follow Compton Road as it bends left. Passing Poynder Close, continue along the lane as it bends right. At the junction with another road, cross over and go over the stile opposite. This Public footpath follows a stream, which is in

fact the upper reaches of Fisher's Brook (which we cross on other walks) before it eventually feeds the Marden. Further on cross stiles that navigate the lane to the farm, next to a bridge over a brook. After a while you will come to a gravel track. Turn left and follow the track for a few yards before taking the PFP on the left, following the edge of field, around the north side of Milestone House (shown on older maps as Lower Penn Cottages). After passing through gates, the path gradually ascends the hill between two hedgerows.

At the top, note the fine, hollowed-out oak on the right. At the junction of tracks, ignore the left one and the stile ahead, and turn right, taking the wide, well-defined, level grass bridleway. After passing by the small wood on the left, the path then skirts an open field, with the top half of the Lansdowne Monument visible directly ahead. We saw red deer here, as the flashes of white on their rumps disappeared into woods.

Go through the small metal gate, where here we saw large deer tracks in the mud. Continue along the well-defined, wide path to the tarmac lane that serves Freeth Farm. Note the old rusting agricultural equipment on the left. Here turn left, following the rough bridleway that passes an adjacent cottage. Futher on, ignore the footpath that goes off ahead and follow the wide track around the left bend. Pass through the two gates as you cross another track, and walk diagonally right across the fields (see public footpath arrow on gatepost for the direction). Make for the tall poplar tree and telegraph pole at the far corner. On arrival at the corner of the field go left through a small gate and take the path that follows the Abberd Brook, on your left. This is a pleasant wooded area, rather forgotten, with fallen trees scattered around. The path all put disappears, but just follow the stream, which soon bends to the right. After this bend, we noted numerous fresh badger setts. The tangled undergrowth and ill-defined path is left behind as you approach the road that goes through Compton Bassett. Turn

right and follow the lane, passing Old Manor Farm on the right, a small pond on the left, as well as a dairy and the old forge. The Lansdowne Monument is again visible in front of you. Further on look for Dove Cottage on the left, with doves in the garden (image left) which nest in an old red telephone box! The White Horse pub will soon be reached, a fitting stop at this stage in the walk (image p. 134). It has a painting of the white horse and the Lansdowne Monument above the entrance, as well as a small painting of the Uffington White Horse. Inside, there are several old photographs of the pub and other local scenes.

Continue south along the road and take the next track on the left (signposted public footpath), which passes by cottages before gradually climbing up the hill onto the chalk. Ignore the public footpath sign on the right a little way up (this is the track we took on walk 11), and keep ascending up this vehicular track, noting the outcrops of chalk on either side of the sunken track— perhaps you may pause to fossil hunt. This sunken way passes through pleasant woodland, but at the top the track levels out and opens up, offering fine views of the Cherhill White Horse and the Lansdowne Monument to the south; look out for the MOD hangars at Lyneham in the distance to the NW. Just beyond the barn, cross the stile, and turn left. You are now walking north along the White Horse Trail, one of Wiltshire's long distance waymarked paths. The scenery for a while is of a flat, open plateau of chalk upland.

The next section of the public footpath crosses an open field so be sure to follow the metal posts that have been erected for that purpose. Head towards the tree line in the distance, noting the chalk fragments and flints underfoot. There are fine views to the west, to Bowood, Calne and Bremhill, and you will soon see the Marlborough Downs on the skyline to the east.

These hills were the source of the huge sarsen stones used in the construction of Avebury, Stonehenge and West Kennet Long Barrow (see Knight 2011). From here, it is amazing how Avebury, the world's largest stone circle, is completely hidden in the valley below, as if by design, to nestle within the body of the ancient Earth Goddess.

Peter descending from the chalk downs through Highway Gully, an ancient wooded track.

The path then passes to the right of the trees, keeping close to the field boundary. Into the next field, the path temporality goes left (west) briefly, before heading across another field; follow the wide yet rough track. Head towards the trees and the barn visible on the other side. On approaching the barn take the track left (west), passing the barn on your right. You may wish to rest a while in the barn, where you can spot the owl box in the roof. Back on the track, continue along until it reaches woodland and starts to descend. This is Highway Gully, good views of which can periodically be had to the left. This lovely, primeval track (image above) becomes sunken, with numerous badger setts and burrows in its banks. This ancient wooded track is a notable feature of one alignment of the Wessex Astrum landscape hexagram; this particular line runs from Holywell (Wotton-under-Edge), through several sites before reaching Beacon Hill, Highway, Stert Pond, Windmill Hill and finally Avebury.

As you exit the gully, continue along the track, which bends right and then

left, down into Highway. On arriving at the road, go straight ahead briefly along a drive to get the best view of St. Peter's church (image left). This is now a private dwelling, but retains a small steeple, weathervane and graveyard. Part of the rood screen was taken from here to the church at Compton Bassett. Retrace your steps to the road and head south, and after some bends take the signposted bridleway on the right. The path keeps to the edge of the field, following a small stream, which is actually a tributary of Cowage Brook. At the far end, ignore the two gates and turn right, where you will soon encounter a small gate which leads to a footbridge over a stream. Over the bridge, the path then skirts the edge of a large field, with hedges on the left. At the far end, go through the gate, pass over the footbridge, and follow the path through two more gates until you reach the road.

Cross the road, and over the stile opposite. From here, head across the field, which offers glimpses of a larger Cowage Brook to the right. Crossing the next stile, Hilmarton Church becomes visible directly ahead. The small copse on the left is often flooded and is the former site of 'Brewer's Pit'. More views of Cowage Brook can be seen on the right, as it passes through woodland. Over more stiles and eventually you will come to a gate, the other side of which is the road and the houses of Hilmarton.

Go straight ahead along the road, heading towards the church tower. Note the chapel on the right which bears the inscription 'Zoar 1924'. Charming,

thatched buildings are soon encountered, and opposite no. 33 take a short detour along the public footpath on the right. A few yards along you will see an arch, which marks the site of the former village limekiln (image left). Retracing your steps to the road, turn right

and you will soon come to the almshouses, with adjoining allotments, on the left. Above one door is a brass plaque, dated 1877, telling how the buildings were built at the expense of William H Poynder, whose armorial initials can be seen on several houses around the village. The five single-storey almshouses (image below) were built in 1877, designed by Henry Weaver, using very distinctive banded fish scale tiled roofs. They were to provide six shillings per week for five residents who had worked on the estate, eligible at the age of 65 years. The Poynder armorial plaque can be seen on each building. Other examples of Weaver's architecture are reflected in the six terraced estate cottages opposite the almshouses.

At the junction, turn right to the church and a little further on you will return to The Duke.

The Victorian almshouses at Hilmarton.

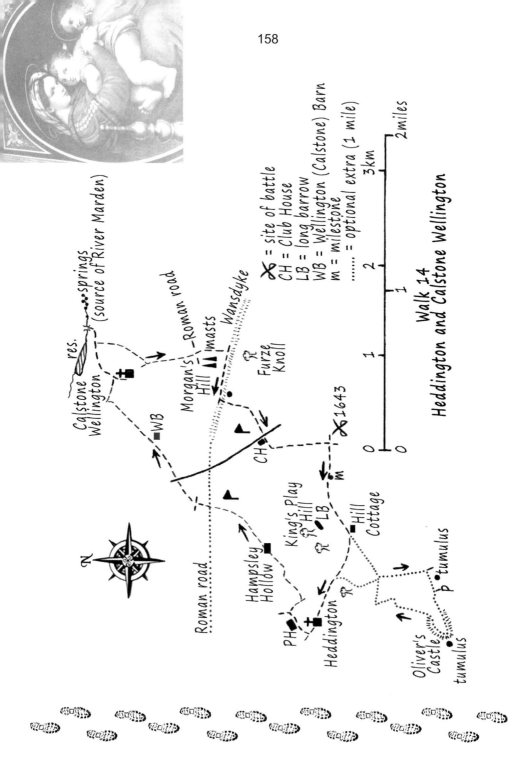

res. ●●●springs
(source of River Marden)

Calstone
Wellington

✝■

Morgan's ▲▲ masts
Hill

Roman road

Wansdyke

WB ■

☈
Furze
Knoll

▲

CH ●

▲

✗ 1643

⚔ = site of battle
CH = Club House
LB = long barrow
WB = Wellington (Calstone) Barn
m = milestone
...... = optional extra (1 mile)

King's Play
☈ Hill
LB

● m

Hill
Cottage ■

Roman road

N

Hampsley
Hollow ■

PH ◆ ✝■
Heddington

☈

●P ●tumulus

Oliver's
Castle ●
tumulus

0   1   2   3km

0   1   2miles

Walk 14
Heddington and Calstone Wellington

Walk 14.

Heddington and Calstone

Summary of Walk 14

Distance: 11km (approx. 7 miles).
Circular or linear: circular.
Start point and end point: The Ivy Inn, Heddington.
Degree of difficulty: moderate incline up from Heddington, and a steep
  incline up to Morgan's Hill. Also long stretches of level walking.
Restrictions: opening hours of the Ivy Inn at Heddington.
Boots/wellies required: stout footwear recommended.
Public transport: bus service L5 - check timetable (no Sunday service).
Wheelchair accessible? – unsuitable for wheelchairs.
Refreshments and toilets: The Ivy Inn, at the start and end of walk.
OS Explorer Map: 157.

This walk offers spectacular views from the chalk downland, visits the
Roman road and Wansdyke, and experiences the atmospheric springs at the
source of the River Marden.

This walk starts and ends at Heddington, a pleasant and well-hidden
hamlet. The name is thought to derive from 'Hedde's–ingtun', land
belonging to the Saxon Hedda. A Roman hoard was found in a local field,
reported by William Stukeley to be, '… a gallon of Roman coin… in an urn
covered with a stone'. Heddington was part of the personal estate of King
Harold prior to the Battle of Hastings. After the Conquest Edward of
Salisbury held the land and in the Domesday Book it is known as 'Edintone',
and later still Lacock Abbey held much of the land until the Reformation. In
1976, Heddington took part in a BBC2 documentary, which followed
village life throughout six months.   As founders of the Calne Environmental

Network, we have happy memories of helping the kindergarten establish a wild flower 'Jubilee Garden' behind the school.

The walk starts at the Ivy Inn (image below and Colour Plate 9). Built in the 17th century, it is a lovely, thatched, 'olde worlde' pub, with an open fire and horse brasses, serving ale direct from casks behind the bar, and

displays of numerous old photographs on the walls.

Leaving the pub entrance, turn left and walk east down Stockley Road. At the junction turn right along Hampsley Rd. Bear left at the fork in the road and continue along a quiet, level lane. Passing Yew Tree Farm, you will come to Yew Tree House, where you can see a well, complete with bucket, and capped by a weathervane with a witch riding a broomstick! Follow the road around the right bend, and a little further you will get views of Calne to the north and northwest, the tall grain silos at Porte Marsh being clearly visible. Further on note the badger setts alongside the road. Follow the bridleway sign as it directs you through the grounds of Hampsley Hollow, an equestrian centre, and beyond this go straight ahead along the gravel track, which gradually ascends on to the chalk hills. Cowslips are plentiful along this stretch during the spring. More badger setts with white heaps of chalk and flints around them reveal that you are now on the chalk. Numerous Peacock and Tortoiseshell butterflies, and Sparrowhawks, may be spotted.

You will soon skirt the golf course and near the top of the hill pause to look back, where you will get a fine view of the steep scarp of King's Play Hill, (a

SSSI) with Heddington occupying the low ground below. In the distance the spire of the church at Derry Hill may be perceived on clear days. Also note the owl box, mounted on a tall post near the track. Just beyond this the course of the old Roman road crosses the track at right angles. On either side it is marked by the hedge line, which in places rises slightly above the field; it is the Roman road that defines the edge of the golf course. Continue straight on, along a track that is enclosed by fences either side. The sound of skylarks overhead is a delight along this stretch. At the intersection of byways keep going straight ahead, where there is soon a welcoming descent down to the road. Calne is again visible in the valley to the left, with the Lansdowne Monument ahead, and Morgan's Hill to the right.

Cross the road (which can be busy) and join the signposted path on the other side. Corn Buntings and Hares may be spotted in this area, as well as

St. Mary's Church, Calstone Wellington.

chalk downland butterflies. The footpath stays close to the edge of the field, and there is a further descent down to Wellington (Calstone) Barn, the new build ahead. Join the tarmac access road, which offers a level walk that eventually gently descends into Calstone. A little way along, note the badger setts in the bank on the right. On reaching the road junction, turn right and pause at the road bridge soon encountered. The large pond in the hollow on the right is fed by springs, the waters of which will soon feed a juvenile River Marden. The stream goes under the road and emerges as a clear bubbling brook. Continue along the road, soon taking the track on the right, signposted to the Old Rectory and the Church. This vehicular track passes through a corridor of high box hedges.

St. Mary's Church is set in a beautiful location, peaceful and alive with birdsong. The tower is short and Cotswold stone tiles cover the roof. At the rear of the church is a welcoming bench midst an idyllic setting. Nearby look for the dark stone monument, mounted with a cross, of Joseph Maundrell, whose family is associated with the former ironworks in Calne. More of his relatives are also laid to rest nearby. Also note some sarsen

stones protruding from under a buttress on the south side of the church; these are often signs that a much older sacred site, even pre-Christian, once stood here.

On entering the porch you come face to face with graffiti, etched into soft stone, some of which is named and bearing dates such as 1630, 1633 and 1688 (image left). The door into the church is very low – duck if you are tall! Inside it was a pleasure to see that the natural stone of the church walls were exposed. Above the nave arch note the unusual carved stone Royal Arms, dated 1740. There is a framed role of vicars which goes right back to 1301, but the appearance of the present church owes much to a major restoration in 1885. On the north side, look for the marble tablet to the Bailey family, the Calne wool merchants and clothiers (p. 82-3). The Michell family vault dates from 1637, and above the pulpit is a marble plaque to Joseph Maundrell, who died in 1926. At the altar, note the wooden reredos, with a scene of the Annunciation. Above this, the east window is dominated by the Crucifixion, with Mary the Mother and Elizabeth (mother of John the Baptist) on the left, and a weeping Mary Magdalene (with flowing golden hair) at the foot of the cross. Just inside the door is a framed painting of a lady in green and red holding an infant, who most would take as Mother Mary and Jesus (see

image left). But much controversial research in recent years suggests that similar depictions (and there are many) may be of Mary Magdalene holding her own child, the father of which was Jesus. Mary Magdalene is frequently shown in green and red, and note the tall anointing jar in the foreground – which is Mary Magdalene's official symbol!

Now retrace your steps to the road, turning right at the pumping station. Ignore the track on the left at the bend, and follow the lane and the bridleway sign, passing the Lodge and Carthorse Cottage. Next to the gate (marked 'South Farm') take the path to the left that descends into very pleasant woodland. Stop on the bridge (image below), midst tranquil woods, above a bubbling stream that cascades over a sluice on the west side. Beyond this the waters flow into a nearby reservoir, built in 1882 to dam the Marden and supply drinking water to Calne. Upstream from the bridge are

the many springs which birth the River Marden; a map of 1773 shows four mills at Calstone. Take time to explore these woods, where you will find several flows of water, small footbridges formed by logs, and multiple springs gushing from the banks, some issuing as miniature waterfalls. It is a profoundly Tolkienesque sanctuary, where clear waters flow beneath moss-covered fallen tree trunks. Early spring is a good time to visit, whilst the nettles still slumber. The water is cool and refreshing to sample.

Two of many springs at Calstone, which are the main source of the River Marden, set amongst a backdrop of tranquil woods.

From the bridge, retrace your steps back up the track, until you take the public footpath that goes off through a gate on the left, opposite the entrance to Carthorse Cottage, (look for a yellow arrow on the fence). This track ascends up to Morgan's Hill, whose two masts rise directly ahead. When you come to two gates, take the right one, and beyond that go through another soon encountered on the left (next to a small copse). Passing through this gate, follow the fence up the right hand side of the field. At the far end, go through the metal gate, next to a fine Wych Elm. Turn right and you will immediately encounter a well-defined track. Go left and you will gradually ascend, walking once again towards the masts on the skyline. At the top of a somewhat steep climb, go through the stile. The wide track that is crossing your path is the Roman road that passes through the southern part of the Calne area on its way from London to Bath. This road (image below) is listed in the 3rd century AD *Antonine Itinerary*, an

inventory of all the important roads in the Empire. We described another section of this road in Walk 12 (see two images on p. 143). The Wessex Ridgeway follows the Roman road along this stretch.

Go through the gate opposite, which allows access to Morgan's Hill Nature Reserve, managed by Wiltshire Wildlife Trust. Neolithic farmers began the process of clearing trees for grazing on the chalk downland, and centuries of sheep grazing since have lead to the development of a distinctive fauna and flora. Look for spring Cowslips and Violets, and in the summer look for Orchids, Fairy Flax, Yellow Rattle, Salad Burnet, Wild Thyme and Birdsfoot Trefoil. The purple heads of Devil's Bit Scabious last into the autumn. On warm days butterflies abound here, such as the Small Tortoiseshell, the Common Blue and the Marbled White. Also look out for short-tailed Field Voles scampering around.

Ascend the slope and go through the gate at the top. From this gate you can look back over the panorama. The ridge on which Bremhill stands is towards the left; Calne, Lower Compton and the solar park are centre-stage, with the Lansdowne Monument rising to the right.

Walk over to the masts. These offer almost 360° vistas. To the south is the prominent copse of beeches called Furze Knoll, with the plateau of Salisbury Plain on the skyline to the left. You can trace the course of Wansdyke, the great Anglo-Saxon defensive/boundary linear earthwork, the snaking course of which you can see going east across open countryside. It runs for 22 miles from Morgan's Hill to beyond Savernake Forest. Further east, you will see

From near the masts on Morgan's Hill, you can look south to Furze Knoll. The dark strip in the middle is Wansdyke, the great Anglo-Saxon earthwork.

Tan Hill rising to around 300m (c.1000ft). One of us has shown that the twin-peaked summit of Morgan's Hill is actually aligned with West Kennet Long Barrow, and may be one of the reasons its long mound is 3° off east-west (Knight 2011, p. 56). The lofty heights of Morgan's Hill was certainly a sacred place in prehistory, as Neolithic finds and Bronze Age tumuli testify; in the Iron Age, the hill marked an important union of the Roman road and Wansdyke.

Walking along the ditch of Wansdyke, Sue shows something of the scale of this 22 mile long earthwork.

Descend to the gate ahead, and going through turn right (west) to join the path that goes along the ditch of Wansdyke, keeping the highest bank to your left; we are quite literally walking in the footsteps of our ancestors. Numerous animal burrows periodically expel heaps of white chalk. Pass through a gate that is set across the ditch and continue ahead.

Harebells and blue butterflies are common here in summer, as the ditch acts as a suntrap. Look out also for Juniper, slow-growing evergreen bushes that are now rare in England. Gradually the path descends and the view opens up to the west. Soon take the gate in the bank on the left, which is a public footpath that traverses the golf course (watch out for flying golf balls!). Head for the Club House, which is visible in the distance.

Cross the road, which may be busy, and beyond the car park entrance take the wide tarmac and gravel track signposted 'Byway'. The next third of a mile is level walking over a flat plateau, even though Morgan's Hill still dominates the landscape behind. At the intersection of wide tracks, take time to pause. For this flat expanse of fields, now quiet and somewhat forgotten, is where the Battle of Roundway Down was fought during the English Civil War. It took place in 1643, between the Parliamentarians (under Puritan Oliver Cromwell) and the Royalists (loyal to Charles I). The battle site is in fact an extended area, including the appropriately named Oliver's Castle. The battle took place on July 13th, following skirmishes around Calne, Chippenham and Devizes. Victory was ultimately claimed by the Royalists, who went on to capture Bristol. Eventually, following his defeat at Preston in 1648, Charles was tried and beheaded in January 1649. Oliver Cromwell himself died in 1658, outliving the deposed King by only nine years.

Around this lonely crossroads, under Morgan's Hill, the Battle of Roundway Down took place in July 1643.

At this junction of tracks turn right (west) and follow the Wessex Ridgeway. A little way along is a milestone on the south side of the track (image below).

This is a relic from the old coaching days, and this track was also used to muster Parliament troops coming up from Rowde prior to the Battle of Roundway Down.

Further along rises King's Play Hill on the right, which is a SSSI. Its summit rises to 230m (754ft) and it hosts prehistoric tumuli and a long barrow. Having passed by two large barns, take the right fork in the road at Hill Cottage. (Should you take the left fork, there is an optional additional walk to Oliver's Castle - see map. This extra section adds another mile to the walk). Having taken the right fork, the road descends through an ancient sunken way, which will eventually take you off the chalk. Note the badger setts high up in the banks, from which white chalk debris have been expelled. Further along, look out for the curious knolls on the left, as well as ridges in the chalk slopes. As the road levels out, follow the bend around to the right, before turning left at the road junction; this will take you to St. Andrew's Church. On the way, note the old converted stables on the right, in the grounds of which stands an old red telephone box!

St. Andrew's (image below) was founded in 1251 by Ela, ward of Richard I, who also built Lacock Abbey in 1232. Inside the tall, slender tower there are six bells, dating from 1605 to 1957. Go through the lych gate (built in 1894) and follow old cobbles to stand outside the 14th century pinnacled north porch. The statue of St. Andrew the Apostle was erected in 1985. He has one foot in the sea and holds broken masts lashed together with rope (image below) in the shape of an 'X'. For he is not only the patron saint of

fishermen, but was crucified on an X-shaped cross called a saltire.

Inside the church the walls are unfortunately lime-washed white, obscuring the stone beneath. In fact the church feels very minimalist – almost Methodist! The south aisle, pillars, north aisle and chancel are c.1300 – 1400s. The bowl of the ornate font is Norman, whilst the wooden cover with the bird is Jacobian. There is a framed list of rectors that goes back to 1298 and a framed and accurate tapestry of Da Vinci's 'The Last Supper'. Most of the windows are plain, although behind the altar are the words, 'God is my light'. An old, intricately carved wooden chair has the Holy Trinity represented by a triangle within a circle.

Exiting through the lych gate, turn left and you will soon come to a sarsen stone, the inscription of which shows it to be a millennium commemoration. Just beyond that is the community-minded 'Book Swop' telephone box, which is full of books to borrow and exchange. Turn right at the junction, signposted to Stockley and Calne. We end our walk where we started, at the Ivy Inn (Colour Plate 9), which affords a friendly welcome for any pilgrim – and good beer straight from the cask!

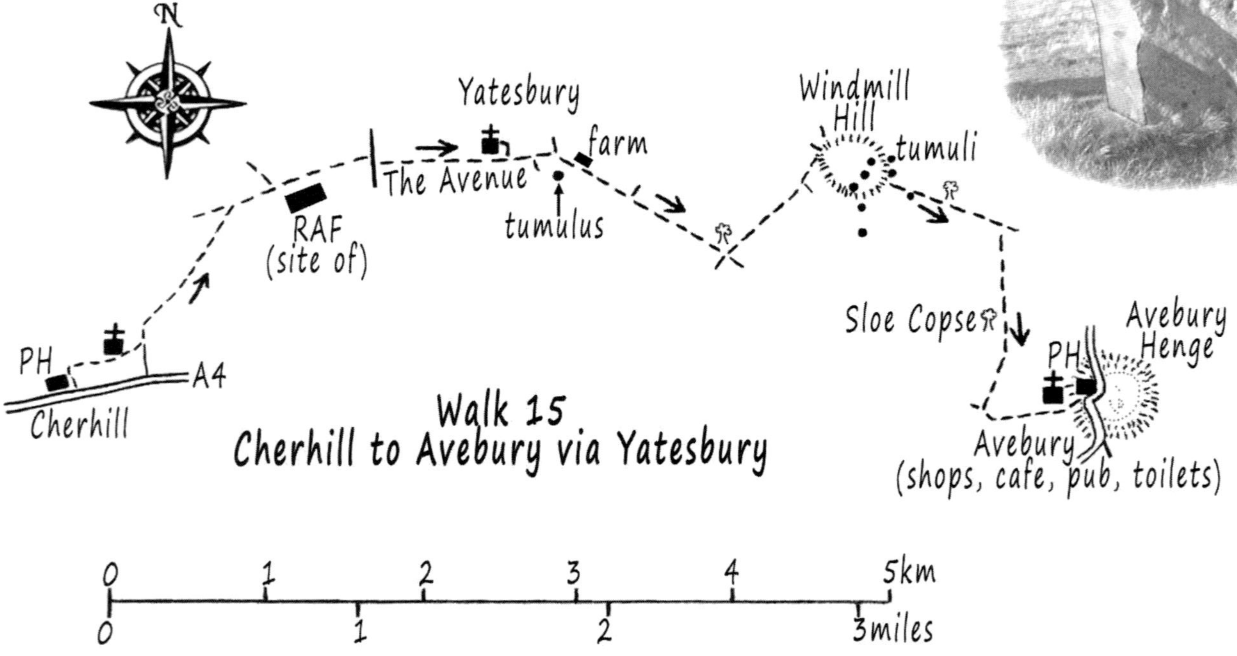

Walk 15
Cherhill to Avebury via Yatesbury

Avebury Henge

Avebury
(shops, cafe, pub, toilets)

PH

Sloe Copse

Windmill Hill

tumuli

farm

Yatesbury

The Avenue

tumulus

RAF
(site of)

Cherhill

A4

PH

N

0   1   1   2   3   4   5km
0   1   2   3miles

Walk 15.
Cherhill to Avebury via Yatesbury.

Summary of Walk 15

Distance: 6.4km (4 miles).
Circular or linear: linear.
Start point: The Black Horse Inn, Cherhill.
End point: Avebury.
Degree of difficulty: easy walking; moderate incline up from Cherhill, but long level stretches thereafter; moderate incline to Windmill Hill.
Restrictions: opening of pub at Cherhill and facilities at Avebury.
Boots/wellies required: stout footwear recommended.
Public transport: bus service L4 - check timetables (no Sunday service).
Wheelchair accessible? – unsuitable for wheelchairs.
Refreshments etc: pub at start & end; café and toilets at Avebury.
OS Explorer Map: 157.

This walk offers isolated rural landscapes, passing through Yatesbury and Windmill Hill, before ending at Avebury, the world's largest Neolithic stone circle and a World Heritage Site.

We begin at the Black Horse, on the A4 at Cherhill, where Walk 11 ended (park on main road if not using the pub). Take the footpath that goes off down the east side of the pub, marked to 'Middle Lane'. On reaching the road go straight ahead down the short lane opposite, turning right at the next junction. Go by the village hall, with its impressive array of solar panels and soon you will reach the church. It is well worth allowing time to inspect the church, details of which can be found on p. 135-6.

Continue east along the lane, going left at the junction (following Cycle Route 403), and then taking the public byway just before the river, marked

'Byway'. This gravel track (an old Anglo-Saxon road) gradually ascends to the chalk plateau, and is lined with Red Campion in spring. At the top, the track levels out and opens up, offering views of the Lansdowne Monument to the right. A WWII brick 'pill box' is soon seen on the right (image below, left), one of several built around the perimeter of the former RAF base. Another can be seen across the field in the distance. Ignore the bridleway that goes off on the left, continuing to follow the 403 signs.

As the track goes through a small wood and skirts the base, there is another pill box next to the track. Just beyond is a clearing in the hedge allowing a peek at one of the old aircraft hangars (image below, right). RAF Yatesbury was opened in the 1st World War and went on to play a major role in WWII. There was formerly a large camp next to the A4 to the south. War graves from both conflicts can be seen in the churchyard (see image p. 173). The aerodrome was closed in 1968, and some of the buildings were demolished soon afterwards. There is an RAF Yatesbury Association.

RAF Yatesbury. Left: one of the pill boxes; Right: an old aircraft hangar (far building).

Continue along this well-defined track, noting another pill box in the field to the left. Turn right at the road, and walk the short distance to the entrance of the old airbase, where a surviving gate post, a chimney and other buildings can be seen close by. Beyond this, at the junction, take the road left, marked 'Yatesbury'. You are now walking along The Avenue, which still marks the Anglo-Saxon road. The Old Rectory is on the left, as is land of the 'Conservation Headland' project. Yatesbury is a fairly isolated village, well 'off the beaten track'. It is listed in the Domesday Book, and sits on a wide chalk plateau on the western edge of the Marlborough Downs and births a head stream of the River Kennet. The area has had almost continuous occupation since Romano-British times, and a Roman farm and a villa was found locally. There was a windmill recorded here in 1309-10, at what is now Yatesbury House Farm, and there were also late-medieval ironworks locally. By 1412 the land was held by St. Mary's Priory in Marlborough, until it passed to the Crown in 1539. The present Yatesbury Manor was built in the late 17th century, with an extensive rebuild in the 19th. There was once a Wesleyan Chapel, built in 1839, and the village also has a history of breeding fine shire horses.

When you come to the next road junction, note the pond and the information board on the left. On the latter are various images of local interest. Take this road left to the church, next to which is the John Stewart Hall, the former school, which has a welcoming bench.

All Saints Church (image left) certainly dates from the 13th century, and possibly from the 12th, suggested by the style of the animal heads set into the doorway. (The church can be accessed by calling one of the numbers in the porch, where instructions on how to obtain the key will be given). At the foot of some of the buttresses protrude large sarsen stones, suggesting an earlier sacred site here. Church records begin in 1291, and the list of rectors in the porch goes back to 1304. The church was built of chalk blocks and freestone, and many of the 13th century medieval features survive, with the addition of the 15th century south porch and west tower. The church was restored in 1854, and has five bells dating from 1636-1931. Note the two scratch sundials on the south side.

Inside offers a pleasant atmosphere, and the Norman font is close to the

Norman font (left), and initialled and dated lead from the old roof (above), inside All Saints Church, Yatesbury.

door. A large black book is located close by, which contains much information on the church and its features. Windows depict John the Baptist, St. Stephen and St. Peter (the latter holding a huge key). Scenes of Christ's life are shown behind the altar. Either side of the altar are intricately painted walls, dating to the 1850s. Underfoot are tiles showing oak leaves and hexagrams, laid in 1854. The organ dates from 1869 and is a rare local example of one made by Holditch of London. Mounted on a wall near the west end is a section of lead from the roof, which is dated 1752 and bears initials (image above). Also look for the copy of the 'Glastonbury Chair', finely carved in wood and dated 1520. Going back outside, you may inspect two rows of white gravestones (image p. 173) associated with RAF Yatesbury, bearing dates between 1918 and 1956.

Leaving the churchyard, retrace your steps down the lane to the road junction and the information board. From here, turn left and continue east along The Avenue, ignoring the 'Byway' sign soon encountered on the right. At the road junction turn right, signposted 'Yatesbury House Farm' and 'Cycle Route 403'. You will soon pass a gate on the left, with polytunnels in the field beyond. These belong to Shumei Natural Agriculture; their farming methods use no chemicals, fertilisers or animal manure, whereby seeking to create '... balanced eco-systems, in which the soil is nurtured to full health'. They have open days, and every year exhibit and sell produce at the Eco Fair on Green Calne Day.

Continue beyond the sign for Yatesbury House Farm, along the permitted path, where you will pass large blocks of sarsen stone, the building material for Avebury and West Kennet Long Barrow. Ignore the entrances to the two cottages either side, carrying straight on along the wide gravel track. Where this track bears left, go straight ahead through the metal gate, signposted 'Bridleway' and '403'. From the gate, and whilst crossing the next field, are

fine views towards the top section of Silbury Hill (image left), and the Lansdowne Monument becomes visible to the south-west. Follow the path that skirts the field, from where we saw deer. Also look out for very hairy caterpillars in the spring; they grow to 5cm (2ins) long, are dark with an orange line and white 'socks' (Colour Plate 13). These belong to the Drinker Moth (ID by Dave Botheridge of the Wilts Branch of Butterfly Conservation); we found them partial to nettles.

After the copse, take the vehicular track left (northeast); this is the White Horse Trail, and this section actually marks the eastern boundary of the Calne Community Area, as well as that of the Avebury World Heritage Site. The track gradually ascends to Windmill Hill, with fine views of Silbury Hill in the valley to the right (southeast). Note the badger setts in the banks further along, marked by ejected white chalk. As the track goes into the woods, ignore the path that goes off at an angle on the right, and a little further, just as you leave the trees behind, take the gate on the right (marked National Trust). Climb the path to the top of the hill, passing mole hills that have likewise expelled tell-tale chalk.

Windmill Hill was an early Neolithic causewayed enclosure, an occupational and ritual site that was first used before 3700 BC. The site covers 21 acres and is 366m (1200ft) in diameter, and excavations revealed large amounts of ritual deposits, such as human and animal bones, antlers, over 20,000 pottery sherds, plus chalk phalli, spheres and figurines. This large gathering place was multi-faceted, and was much more than a defensive earthwork or trading post. It hosted major seasonal feasts and ceremonies, involving many hundreds of people. Several Bronze Age tumuli still jut out of the hill today, a token of the importance of the site thousands of years ago, and proof that its importance spanned a long period of time.

At the top, make for the largest of several tumuli directly ahead. This ancient burial mound offers an uplifting 360° panorama, as Skylark song fills the air. Silbury Hill rises like a whale in the valley to the south. Although it is the tallest Neolithic monument in Europe, it is positioned in a dip, seemingly built with great humility for the higher, encircling natural hills. Note the slender strip of West Kennet Long Barrow beyond, and how it appears to touch the side of Silbury Hill, an intentional Neolithic alignment of great precision (see p. 29 of Knight 2011, and image below, left). To the right rises Knoll Down, and further west Cherhill Down, capped by the Lansdowne Monument. Further west and northwest the flat plateau stretches away, with Yatesbury mainly hidden within trees. To the east the skyline is dominated by the Marlborough Downs, with numerous tumuli. Avebury is well concealed in the valley to the southeast, with no hint that the world's largest stone circle is even there. To the left of Silbury Hill rises Waden Hill, a phallic-shaped ridge pointing towards Avebury's mighty henge/stone circle (Knight 2011, p. 7).

Left: from Windmill Hill, note how West Kennet Long Barrow appears to touch the slopes of Silbury Hill, at the top ledge. Right: Peter dowsing the earth energies on Windmill Hill.

Windmill Hill is also one of those places where the Michael and Mary energy currents of the famous St. Michael Line cross (see Miller and Broadhurst, 1989). We found the currents to be crossing midst a thick patch of nettles (image above, right). Dowsing rods twitched and swung as the pulse of Mother Earth was experienced. We have found that most sacred sites are positioned where earth energies can be dowsed and strongly felt. Did our ancestors likewise experience these ethereal forces?

Beyond the barrow follow the path east to the gate ahead. There is an information board here, including a map pointing out the archaeology. Now walk ahead following the White Horse Trail, through a field we found to be

full of Vetch and we spotted Orange Tip butterflies (Colour Plate 13). The tower of Avebury church now becomes visible to the right. The grass path gradually descends into the river valley of the Winterbourne, one of the head waters of the River Kennet. At the bottom, go through the field boundary and just the other side cross the stile on the right (marked 'Avebury 1 mile'). Across the next couple of fields the river runs parallel to the east. Cross over more stiles, and along here you may catch glimpses of the banks of Avebury Henge to the left.

At the far end of the field cross over two more stiles, and continue on to another. Avebury Manor can now be seen to the left. Go over the footbridge that crosses a stream, turning left towards the gate. You can look back north from here and see the tumuli on Windmill Hill on the skyline. Go left

The carved Norman font in St James.

at the tarmac path, crossing the river via the small bridge made of sarsen stones (image above). Two welcoming benches beyond afford a great view of Silbury Hill to the south. Continue to the church. St. James is mainly Norman, with a 15th century tower, and yet an Anglo-Saxon nave survives. There are many fine treasures inside, including a rood screen, a stone coffin from the Benedictine Abbey, depictions of the apostles on gilded panels, some Norman tiles, and fine windows. The Norman font (which may have a Saxon origin) is well worth examination, as it has two dragons carved into it (image above), which some writers see as the Michael and Mary 'dragon lines' that flow through Avebury.

Above: experiencing the stones of Avebury. Below: the Henge Shop, which stocks many books about Avebury.

There are many things to see in Avebury, such as the restored Manor, museums, café, pub, village pond and the wondrous Henge Shop. But it is the stone circle that is the star attraction. It is the world's largest, comprising huge stones of Neolithic age, with dowsable energies, and an impressive bank and ditch. Many of the stones show simulacra, such as heads, faces and creatures, which may have been a factor in the selection of the stones over 4,000 years ago. There are also several astronomical and landscape alignments, some of which involve West Kennet Long

Barrow (Knight 2011, p. 170-4). There are some excellent books on the various aspects of Avebury, and a good selection can be found in The Henge Shop (image above) and the National Trust shop. The authors run tours and dowsing/shamanic workshops at Avebury (details on our website).

The bus back to Calne (service L4) can be caught at the Red Lion pub.

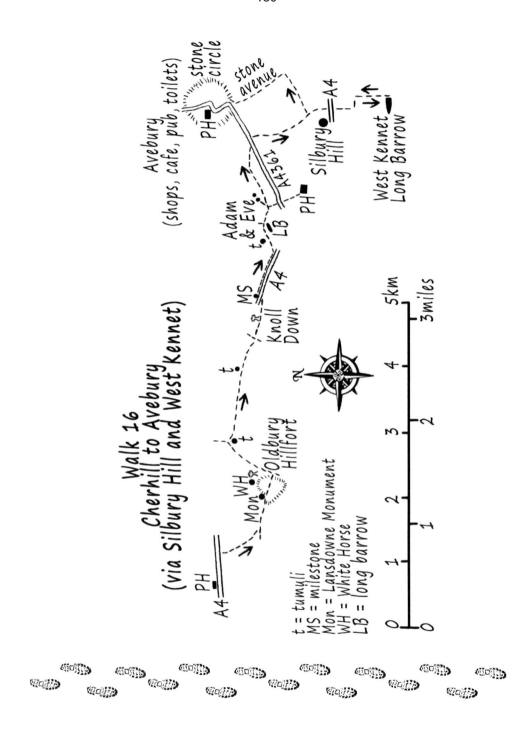

Walk 16
Cherhill to Avebury
(via Silbury Hill and West Kennet)

Avebury
(shops, cafe, pub, toilets)

stone circle
stone avenue

t = tumuli
MS = milestone
Mon = Lansdowne Monument
WH = White Horse
LB = long barrow

5km
3miles

Walk 16.
Cherhill to Avebury via Silbury Hill
& West Kennet Long Barrow

Summary of Walk 16

Distance: 12km (approx. 7½ miles).
Circular or linear: linear.
Start point: The Black Horse Inn, Cherhill.
End point: Avebury.
Degree of difficulty: mostly easy, but moderate incline up from
    Cherhill, and short but steep walk up Waden Hill near the end.
Restrictions: opening hours of pub at Cherhill and facilities at Avebury.
Boots/wellies required: stout footwear recommended.
Public transport: bus service L4 - check timetable (no Sunday service).
Wheelchair accessible? – unsuitable for wheelchairs.
Refreshments etc: pub and café at start & end; and toilets at Avebury.
OS Explorer Map: 157.

Walk east (uphill) along the A4 from the Black Horse. Cross over the road and take the bridleway that is almost opposite Park Lane. The last building on the left (dated 'c.1726' to the right of the door) used to be the Bell Inn, a former coaching stop. At the start of the bridle track there are two information boards, one about Cherhill Down, the other describing Wiltshire's white horses. Take this gently ascending track, which offers good views of the Cherhill White Horse on the left. The chalk figure was cut in 1780, and is the second oldest of Wiltshire's chalk horses, the third oldest in England. It was scoured under the direction of Dr Christopher Alsop of Calne, who designed it to be elongated so as to resemble the horses of the artist George Stubbs, who was a friend of Alsop. At one time it had glass bottles for eyes! (See p. 140 for more details, and Colour Plate 10.)

You will soon see chalk underfoot and in the banks further up, where the

track becomes sunken. Ignore the stile on the left, although this offers good views to the white horse to the east. A notice tells us that the National Trust manages the land (image left), which is also an SSSI. Further on the view opens up, and after going through the gate ahead, bear left and walk in the direction of the Lansdowne Monument (image p. 141). There are also good views west to Morgan's Hill, and to the north in the valley below are the buildings of the former RAF base at Yatesbury. The flora can be stunning along this stretch, with blue Bugles and yellow Cowslips in spring, and Orchids, round-headed Rampion, Thistles, Toadflax, and Field Fleawort in summer, as well as stunning butterflies, such as the Adonis Blue and Marsh Fritillary.

There are information boards on the far side of the monument. From here take the well-defined track to the right of the obelisk into Oldbury Castle, the Iron Age hillfort. Note the undulating ramparts below on the right (see aerial image, p. 142). Go out through the east entrance, and beyond the banks and ditches you should turn left and follow the gravel vehicular track which goes northwards and downhill. This is both the route of the White Horse Trail and the Wessex Ridgeway. The track passes to the right of the hilltop copse, from which we heard the tapping of Woodpeckers. As you descend, note Silbury Hill to the east, beyond the rise of Knoll Down. Go through the gate near the barn, beyond which are fine views to the northwest, where the Cotswolds rise on the skyline. Below in the valley is the best view of the dark hangar of the former RAF base at Yatesbury, which we passed on Walk 15 (image p. 172).

The track soon passes to the left of a large Bronze Age burial mound, or tumulus. Just as the main road comes into view, take the track off to the right, which passes around the back of the mound. You are now walking the route of the Old Bath Road, a pleasant level walk that runs parallel with the newer A4 route below. Further on, avoid the wide field entrance, keeping to the right. The track runs along a natural ridge which gives fine views either side. Ahead, the Marlborough Downs rise on the skyline and you may get glimpses of a white patch at the north end of the scarp; this is the

Broad Hinton White Horse, which dates from 1835.

Just beyond a rise, with its sunken track, note the Bronze Age tumulus on the left, just beyond the gate (image left). Further on, as you approach the tall trees on Knoll Down, the path veers to the right of them, but you can soon bear left to enter the wood. This lovely Beech wood is dissected by the old coach road, and offers Bluebells in spring and welcome shade on warmer days. The hill is a place of peaceful and powerful dowsable energies connected with the St. Michael Line, which we think is what gives the wood its magical feeling (see Miller and Broadhurst, 1989, p. 202). Next to the car park, a pleasant enough place to pause and rest, you can get views across the gallops; Milk Hill and Tan Hill straddle the southern skyline.

Left: the Beech wood on Knoll Down. Right: the milestone on the main road.

At the far end of the car park cross the A4 to scrutinize the old coach road milestone opposite. It is made of fossiliferous Cotswold stone, and inscriptions inform us it is 82 miles to London, yet only 5 to Calne. From here follow the tarmac path east alongside the A4 road, which gradually descends to the Beckhampton roundabout, noting Silbury Hill rising in front of you. Well before the roundabout, take the track going off to the left, just before the 'horse and rider 200yds' sign. This track is signposted 'Windmill Hill and Avebury'.

Pass by the metal gates of The Grange and you will soon come to the Longstones (or Beckhampton) Long Barrow, a long and lofty Neolithic mound (image left). I have previously shown how the mound is in a solstice alignment with West Kennet Long Barrow and other local sacred sites (Knight 2011, p. 171). Nicholas Mann has also suggested astronomical alignments with the nearby Adam and Eve stones (Mann, 2011, p. 159-60). Our ancient ancestors were clearly positioning mounds very mindfully on the landscape. The barrow also has dowsable Earth energies associated with the St. Michael Line (Miller and Broadhurst 1989, p. 203). No human remains were found here, but ox skulls and deer antlers gave an age of around 3100BC for this impressive Neolithic mound.

Continuing ahead you will soon see the two huge megaliths that are 'Adam and Eve' in the field beyond (image below). Take the track to the right and you will come to a stile allowing access to the stones. These are the survivors of a megalithic avenue that went into Avebury. Adam and Eve were also

originally part of a 'cove' of six large stones that were aligned astronomically to the mid-winter solstice and the rising of the brightest star Sirius during the Neolithic, around 5,000 years ago (see Mann 2011); from the stones, the Beckhampton Long Barrow also marked the setting of Sirius. Powerful energies associated with the St. Michael Line also flow through the stones (Miller and Broadhurst 1989). From here the burial mounds on Windmill Hill are on the skyline to the north (left side of image above).

From this stile there are two options. If you would like to visit the Waggon and Horses pub at Beckhampton, 5 minutes walk to the south, then take the road south from the stile, cross the A4361, continue along the footpath beyond to the pub. The Waggon and Horses, originally called the Black Bear, was built in 1669 as a coaching inn, and is constructed of sarsen stones. It was given its present name in 1823, due to the road (now the A4) being used by drovers for driving their livestock between Bristol and London. The pub offered accommodation, stables and a smithy. The inn is mentioned by Charles Dickens in his 'Pickwick Papers'– he passed this way on his visits to Bath. Two ghosts are said to haunt the public bar, and outside the sounds of a spectral coach and horses are reportedly heard.

If you have been to the pub, retrace your steps back to the Adam and Eve stile. Now, take the tarmac lane east to Avebury Trusloe. The village features some pretty thatched cottages incorporating sarsen stones. At the crossroads, continue ahead down Frog Lane. Opposite Long Furrow Cottage take the stile on the right. Cross the field diagonally left, noting the hollows, ridges and bumps which are the remains of a medieval settlement. Silbury Hill comes into view as the stile at the far side is approached. At the road, turn left (east) and walk the short distance to New Bridge. This was built in 1950 and spans the Winterbourne, which will soon become the River Kennet. A further 45m (50 yds) beyond the bridge take the bridleway on the right, through the gate marked with a blue arrow.

This path follows the stream south towards Silbury Hill (image below), which looms ever larger. Beyond the sarsen and brick footbridge (do not

cross this), West Kennet Long Barrow becomes visible on a low ridge directly ahead, a long dark streak on the landscape. Further stiles and gates take you to the road (A4). Just before, there are fine views of Silbury Hill. This truly is one of the wonders of prehistory, the tallest Neolithic mound ever constructed in Europe. It was built in three stages between 2900BC and 2350BC, eventually comprising 350,000 cubic metres (12.4 million cubic ft). It is a pyramid, rising to 40m (130ft) above the valley floor, constructed of earth, flint and chalk, and would have originally gleamed white in the landscape. Much has been written about the monument, and it has been covered by one of the authors regarding its links with West Kennet Long Barrow (Knight 2011). The fact that the fields around Silbury regularly flood (Colour Plate 15) may have been calculated, to enhance its 'feminine' symbolism. A Roman settlement and temple were later built in the low area to the east of the mound.

Cross over the road to the lay-by, where you will see West Kennet Long Barrow on the skyline. Access into the field beyond is at the east end, next to a cottage. Just inside the field you will see an information board, describing the Avebury World Heritage Site. Follow the gravel track to the small bridge over the River Kennet, left through the kissing gate, right at the solitary oak, ascending the hill along a well-trodden path.

As you approach the summit, the 100m (c.328ft) long mound of the long barrow can be appreciated. Take time here to absorb the ancient landscape, which stretches out before you in every direction. One of us has written the

The stones of West Kennet Long Barrow.

definitive guide to West Kennet Long Barrow, detailing the astronomy, excavations, geometry, landscape alignments, dowsing energies, and much more (Knight 2011). The protracted mound is impressive even today, and the dark chambers behind the tall stones (Colour Plate 16) seem to lure us in, as they did our ancestors 5,500 years ago. The chambers were always a place for the living as well as the dead, a place of initiation and rites of passage. Inside look for faces in the stones, which were part of the shamanic aspect of the site; this is a place where imaginations were let out to play, and contact was sought with the ancestors; nothing has changed. We hold regular, experiential events here.

Retrace your steps back to the A4 road, cross the road and head back north (signposted 'Avebury 1 mile') along the path that follows the stream. At the first field boundary, do not go through the gate this time, rather turn right and follow the fence line to the top of Waden Hill. At the top of the hill, turn back to admire the view. Silbury Hill is well below you, which is not normally the case, demonstrating how the mound was not intended to protrude above the natural hills. Beyond is Morgan's Hill (look for the two masts). To the east, large Beech clumps envelop ancient burial mounds, some of which are astronomically aligned when viewed from West Kennet Long Barrow (Knight 2011, p. 186–8).

Continue downhill, noting the offering (or 'cloutie') Hawthorn on the left, adorned with ribbons and other objects. West Kennet Avenue becomes visible below; this double row of stones of Late Neolithic age weaves, snake-like, across the lower ground (see back cover). At the road, take the gate that gives you access to the stones, and proceed up the avenue, looking out for faces and

The ancient stone avenue that wends its way to Avebury.

creatures in the stones. Just beyond the crest of the rise, pause between the last pair of stones. The one on the left is a classic lozenge/diamond shaped 'female' stone, whereas the one on the right is a phallic-shaped 'male' stone. You can see Avebury church ahead, and to the left Morgan's Hill; the seemingly ever-present Lansdowne Monument is on the skyline. Follow the concrete markers down to the road, cross over, and go under the Beeches into Avebury stone circle. The two huge megaliths in front of you are one of the four ancient entrances to Avebury, to where the stone avenue directed prehistoric pilgrims. The stone on the left has a seat, and should you choose to sit on it (image p. 179), it will probably be the oldest chair you will ever sit on!

We have come to the end of our offering of 16 pilgrimages through Calne's heritage and landscape. We hope you have enjoyed walking, quite literally, in the footsteps of your ancestors.

Acknowledgements

We gratefully acknowledge the help of many people, both known and unknown, during this project. We particularly thank Roger Walters; Sue Boddington and the other volunteers at the Heritage Centre; the Wilts and Berks Canal Trust; Calne Library; the trustees of Marden House; The Calne Project, Mike Rawle and other volunteers at St Mary's; the staff of the Visitor Information Centre in Bank House; Dave Botheridge; and Peter Treloar, whose books on Calne were invaluable. Thanks also to Brian R Marshall, for posting an image on Wiki.

Resources

Stone Seeker Tours: www.stoneseeker.net
Calne Heritage Centre, New Road: www.calneheritage.co.uk
Calne Springs: www.calnewiltshire.com
Calne Town Council: www.calne.gov.uk
Visitor Information Centre, Bank House, The Strand, Calne: 01249 814000
Calne Library: 01249 813128.
The Community Hub, High St. Calne: 01249 813747
The Henge Shop, Avebury: www.hengeshop.com
Wiltshire Wildlife: www.wiltshirewildlife.org
Local Connect2 bus services: www.bookaride.net

References and Further Reading

Beale, Norman, *Joseph Priestley in Calne*, 2008, Hobnob.

Burl, Aubrey, *Prehistoric Avebury,* 2002 ed., Yale.

Calne Project, The, *The Calne Trail.* Calne Civic Society.

Calne Project, The, *A Walker's Guide to Calne.*

Knight, Peter, *Dorset Pilgrimages - A Millennium Handbook* (with Mike Power), 2000, Power Publications.

Knight, Peter, *Thirteen Moons - Conversations with the Goddess,* 2007 (& 2012 ed.), Stone Seeker.

Knight, Peter, (with Perrott, Toni), *The Wessex Astrum - Sacred Geometry in a Mystical Landscape,* 2008, Stone Seeker.

Knight, Peter, *West Kennet Long Barrow - Landscape, Shamans and the Cosmos,* 2011, Stone Seeker.

Knight, Peter, *The Cerne Giant - Landscape, Gods and the Stargate,* 2013, Stone Seeker.

Mann, Nicholas R, *Avebury Cosmos,* 2011, O Books.

Miller, Hamish, and Broadhurst, Paul, *The Sun and the Serpent,* 1989, Pendragon.

Pollard, Joshua, and Reynolds, Andrew, *Avebury – The Biography of a Landscape*, 2002, Tempus.

Rose, David E, *Calne Artist Town Guide*, 2001, Rose Art.

Small, Doug, *Wilts and Berks Canal Revisited*, 2010, The History Press.

Treloar, Peter Q, *Calne In Camera,* 1974. Calne Borough Council.

Treloar, Peter Q, *Calne In Focus*, 1984, Calne Town Council.

Treloar, Peter Q, *Greetings From Calne*, 1988, Calne Town Council.

Treloar, Peter Q, *Around Calne in Old Photographs*, 1990, Alan Sutton.

Treloar, Peter, *Calne Revisited,* 1999, Calne Town Council.

Treloar, Peter Q, *Calne's Heritage*, 2010, The History Press.

About the Authors

Sue Wallace has been a qualified holistic therapist since 1994, using a blend of shiatsu, reiki, acupressure, dowsing, and nutritional and lifestyle advice. Some of Sue's earliest childhood memories are of a deep connection to Nature, which instilled a passion for ecology and environmental issues. Sue discovered dowsing in 1999 with the Surrey Dowsers and went on to be their Chairman from 2005-9. She now lives in Calne, where she grows her own vegetables, and she is the co-founder of the Calne Environmental Network.

Peter Knight is the author of 9 books on sacred sites and ancient wisdom, a freelance writer, and is well known for his lively and enthusiastic workshops, convention lectures and field trips about topics relating to our heritage. He was co-founder of the Dorset Earth Mysteries Group, is an Honorary Member of the Dorset Dowsers, and is on the committee of the Wyvern Dowsers. He instigated and still chairs the Convention of Alternative Archaeology and Earth Mysteries, held annually in Wiltshire and which is now in its 11th year. He has appeared on radio and TV, such as on Channel 4 with Monty Don. He lives in Calne and is co-founder of the Calne Environmental Network (www.calne-environmental-network.org.uk).